John Brimhall's THEORY NOTEBOOK

Complete

PART 1

D1608532

32618

John Brimhall's THEORY NOTEBOOK Complete

PART 2

John Brimhall's THEORY NOTEBOOK Complete

PART 3

lesson **1**

THE STAFF

STAFF

The lines and spaces on which music is written

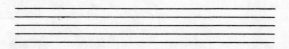

Notes are placed on both the lines and the spaces of the staff to show the pitch of the notes. The higher the note on the staff, the higher the pitch (high or low sound).

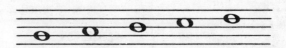

This is a note on a LINE

This is a note on a SPACE

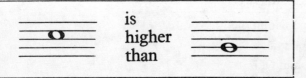
is higher than

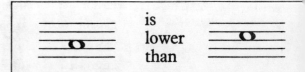
is lower than

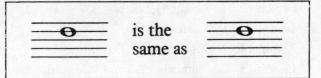
is the same as

• •

Indicate whether the second note is higher, lower or the same as the first note of each set.

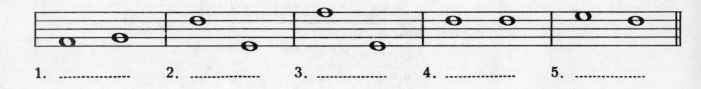

1. .... 2. .... 3. .... 4. .... 5. ....

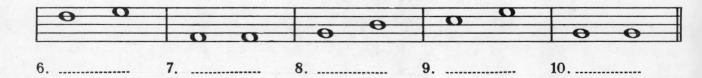

6. .... 7. .... 8. .... 9. .... 10. ....

NOTE: Answers to all Quiz Questions may be found in text material preceding the Quiz.

THE LINES OF THE TREBLE STAFF

This is a **TREBLE CLEF**

A staff with a Treble Clef sign is called a Treble Staff. High notes are placed on the Treble Staff.

The lines of the Treble Staff are

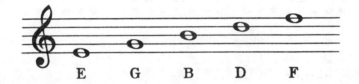

A saying to help you remember the lines of the Treble Staff is:

Every **G**ood **B**oy **D**oes **F**ine

• •

Write in the letter names of these notes.

Draw the correct line note over each letter name.

THE SPACES OF THE TREBLE STAFF

The spaces of the
Treble Staff are:

To help you remember the spaces of the
Treble Staff, they spell FACE.

• •

Write in the letter names of these notes.

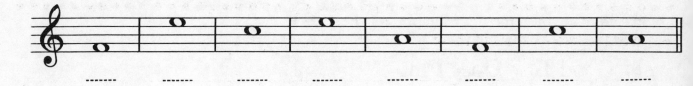

------   ------   ------   ------   ------   ------   ------   ------

Draw the correct space note over each letter name.

Spell the following words with space notes.

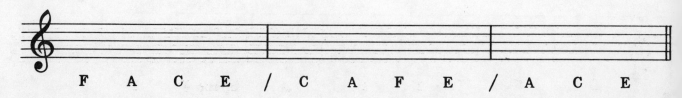

DOUBLE BAR

DOUBLE BAR

At the end of every song or other
musical composition is a sign which means
"the END". It is composed of a narrow
bar line and a wide bar line.

There is also a Double Bar with two narrow
bar lines, designating the end of part of a
composition, but not the final close.

● ●

Write in the letter names of these notes.

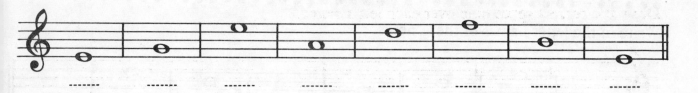

Draw a note over each letter name.

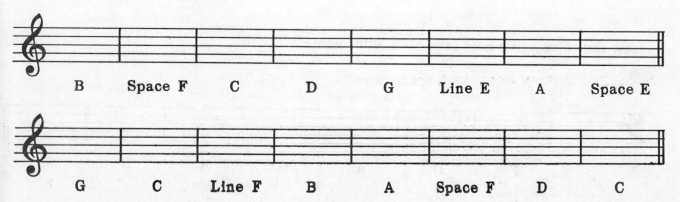

B   Space F   C   D   G   Line E   A   Space E

G   C   Line F   B   A   Space F   D   C

THE LINES OF THE BASS STAFF

This is a BASS CLEF

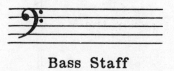

A staff with a Bass Clef sign is called a Bass Staff. Low notes are placed on the Bass Staff.

Bass Staff

The lines of the Bass Staff are

G   B   D   F   A

A saying to help you remember the lines of the Bass Staff is:

Good **B**oys **D**eserve **F**un **A**lways

• •

Write in the letter names of these notes.

------   ------   ------   ------   ------   ------   ------   ------

Draw the correct line note over each letter name.

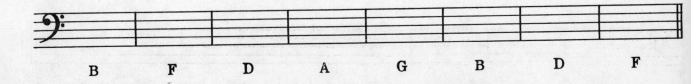

B   F   D   A   G   B   D   F

lesson 6

THE SPACES OF THE BASS STAFF

The spaces of the
Bass Staff are

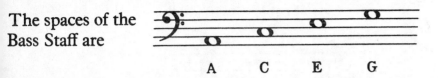

A   C   E   G

A saying to help you remember the spaces of the
Bass Staff is:

All **C**ows **E**at **G**rass

• •

Write in the letter names of these notes.

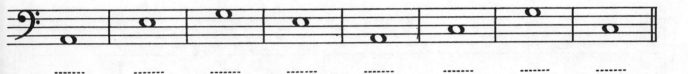

------   ------   ------   ------   ------   ------   ------   ------

Draw the correct space note over each letter name.

G   A   E   C   A   C   G   E

Spell the following words with space notes.

A G E / A C E / C A G E

THE GREAT STAFF

GREAT STAFF

The Great Staff is composed
of a Treble Staff and a
Bass Staff joined by a Brace.
High notes and low notes
are placed on the Great Staff.

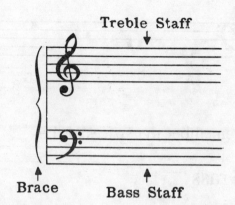

• •

Write in the letter names of these notes.

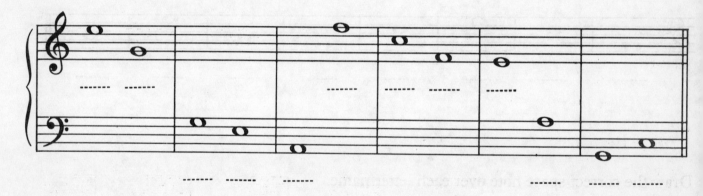

Draw the correct note over each letter name.

lesson 8

WRITING PRACTICE-CLEFS and BRACES

Draw Treble Clefs

Draw Bass Clefs

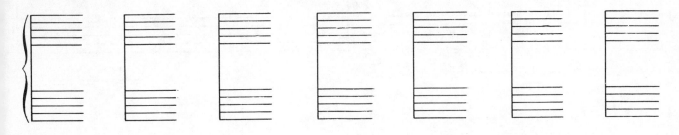

Draw Braces

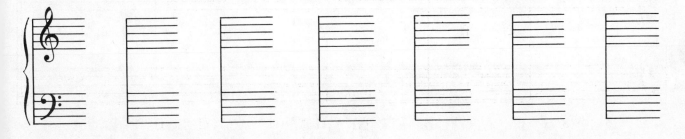

Draw Braces and Clefs

LEGER LINES

LEGER LINES
are lines added
above or below a staff.

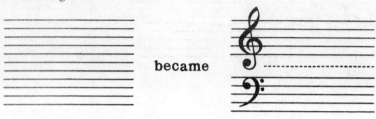
← Leger line

In the early history of music, the Great Staff had eleven
lines. The middle line was later removed, in order to make
reading easier. Now, when that middle line (middle C) is
needed, a short piece of the middle line is drawn and
called a leger line.

became

Middle C

• •

Fill in the words that these notes spell.

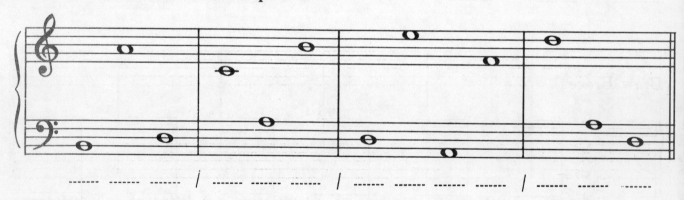

------- ------- ------- / ------- ------- ------- / ------- ------- ------- ------- / ------- ------- -------

Draw the notes that these words spell.

B A G G A G E / B E G / C A G E / F A D E

REVIEW OF GREAT STAFF

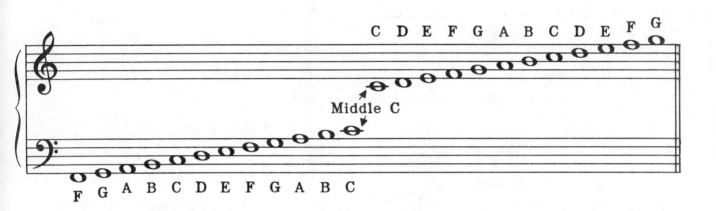

• •

Draw the following notes found on the Great Staff.

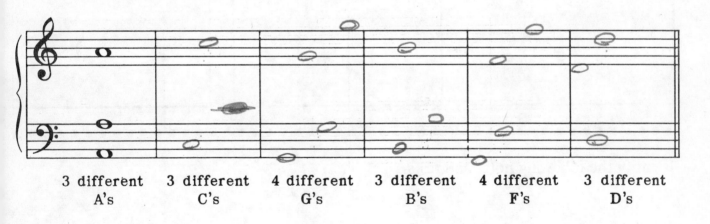

| 3 different A's | 3 different C's | 4 different G's | 3 different B's | 4 different F's | 3 different D's |

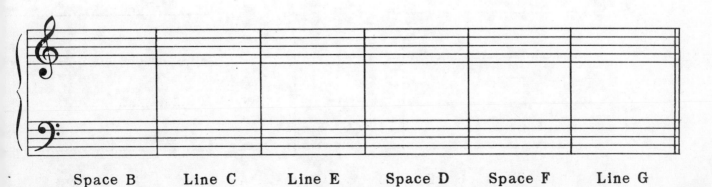

| Space B | Line C | Line E | Space D | Space F | Line G |

NOTES AND RESTS

There are various kinds of NOTES designed to show
the duration or time value of a musical sound.
RESTS are symbols indicating a definite duration or time
value of silence.

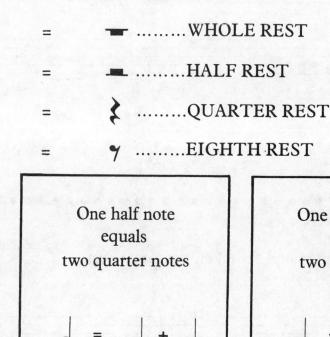

WHOLE NOTE......... 𝅝 = ▬ ....WHOLE REST
(Semi-breve)

HALF NOTE......... 𝅗𝅥 = ▬ ....HALF REST
(Minim)

QUARTER NOTE ... ♩ = 𝄽 ....QUARTER REST
(Crochet)

EIGHTH NOTE..... ♪ = 𝄾 ....EIGHTH REST
(Quaver)

One whole note equals two half notes	One half note equals two quarter notes	One quarter note equals two eighth notes
𝅝 = 𝅗𝅥 + 𝅗𝅥	𝅗𝅥 = ♩ + ♩	♩ = ♪ + ♪

• •

Identify the following notes and rests.

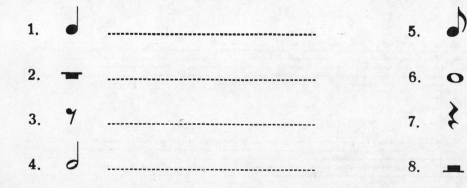

1. ♩ ....

2. ▬ ....

3. 𝄾 ....

4. 𝅗𝅥 ....

5. ♪ ....

6. 𝅝 ....

7. 𝄽 ....

8. ▬ ....

WRITING PRACTICE—NOTES

Draw Whole Notes

Draw Half Notes

Draw Quarter Notes

Draw Eighth Notes

Draw Beamed Eighth Notes

NOTE AND REST VALUES

In most music the fundamental beat is assigned to the Quarter Note. If the Quarter Note gets one beat (count), then the following is true:

QUARTER NOTE	(♩)	=	1 count
HALF NOTE	(♩)	=	2 counts
WHOLE NOTE	(o)	=	4 counts
EIGHTH NOTE	(♪)	=	1/2 count

and
TWO EIGHTH NOTES (♫) = 1 count

• •

How many counts do each of the following get ?

1. ♩ _____

2. o _____

3. ♩ _____

4. 𝄾 _____

5. ♫ _____

6. ▬ _____

7. 𝄽 _____

8. ♩ + ♩ _____

9. ▬ _____

10. ♪ _____

Draw the following notes and rests:

1. A 1 count Note..........

2. A 1/2 count Rest.........

3. A 2 count Note..........

4. A 1 count Rest..........

5. A 4 count Note..........

6. A 2 count Rest..........

7. A 1/2 count Note..........

8. A 4 count Rest..........

CHART OF RELATIVE NOTE AND REST VALUES

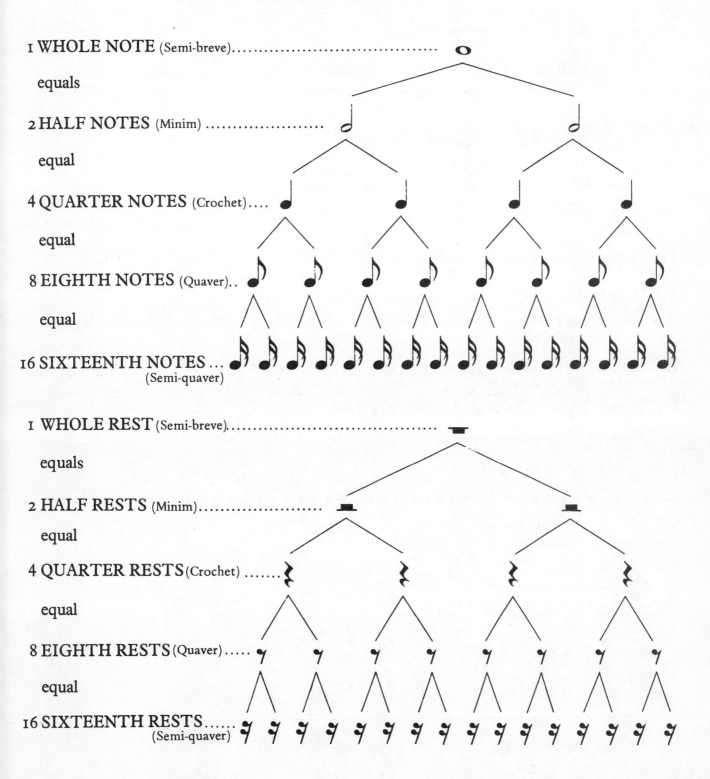

1 WHOLE NOTE (Semi-breve).....................................

equals

2 HALF NOTES (Minim).....................

equal

4 QUARTER NOTES (Crochet)....

equal

8 EIGHTH NOTES (Quaver)..

equal

16 SIXTEENTH NOTES ...
(Semi-quaver)

1 WHOLE REST (Semi-breve)...............................

equals

2 HALF RESTS (Minim)....................

equal

4 QUARTER RESTS (Crochet).......

equal

8 EIGHTH RESTS (Quaver).....

equal

16 SIXTEENTH RESTS......
(Semi-quaver)

DOTTED NOTES

A dot after a note adds $\frac{1}{2}$ to the value
of that note.

The Half Note (♩) = 2 counts

The Dotted Half Note $(\text{♩}.)$ = 3 (2 + 1) counts

The Quarter Note (♩) = 1 count

The Dotted Quarter Note $(\text{♩}.)$ = $1\frac{1}{2}$ ($1 + \frac{1}{2}$) counts

The Whole Note (o) = 4 counts

The Dotted Whole Note $(\text{o}\cdot)$ = 6 (4 + 2) counts

The Eighth Note (♪) = $\frac{1}{2}$ count

The Dotted Eighth Note $(\text{♪}.)$ = $\frac{3}{4}$ ($\frac{1}{2} + \frac{1}{4}$) count

• •

How many counts do the following get ?

1. ♩. _____ 3

2. ♪ ♩ _____ $1\frac{1}{2}$

3. ♩ ♩ _____ 3

4. ♩. _____ $1\frac{1}{2}$

5. o _____ 4

6. ▬ _____ 4

7. 𝄽 ♪ _____ $\frac{1}{4} + \frac{1}{8}$

8. o · _____ 6

9. ♩ ♩. _____ $3\frac{1}{2}$

10. ♩· ♩ _____ 4

MEASURE, 4/4 TIME SIGNATURE

Counts are grouped together to form measures.
Measures may contain two, three, four or more
counts. Measures are separated by bar lines.

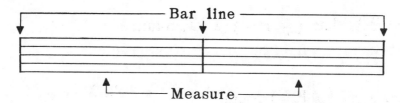

TIME SIGNATURE

The grouping of counts into measures is indicated
by the time signature, which appears at the beginning
of each song.

The top number of the Time Signature tells how many
counts in each measure.
The bottom number tells what kind of note is to
receive one count.

$\frac{4}{4}$ = 4 counts in each measure.
Each quarter note (♩) gets one count.

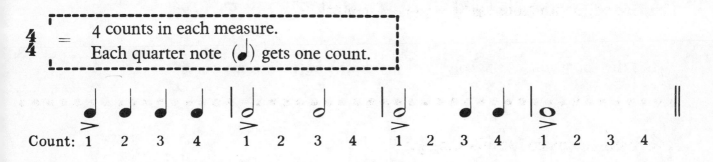

Count: 1 2 3 4 | 1 2 3 4 | 1 2 3 4 | 1 2 3 4

ACCENT SIGN

This sign directs the player to give
special emphasis to the note. On the
piano, strike the note a little harder.

in 4/4 time the 1st count of each measure is Accented.

C = Common Time. This sign is often used as a substitute for 4/4 time.

3/4 TIME

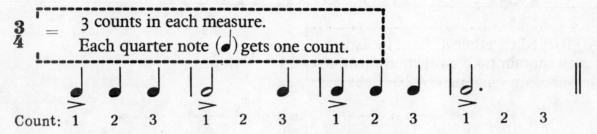

$\frac{3}{4}$ = 3 counts in each measure.
Each quarter note ($\quarternote$) gets one count.

Count: 1   2   3   1   2   3   1   2   3   1   2   3

In 3/4 time the 1st count of each measure is accented.

● ●

Write the counts under the notes.

1. $\frac{3}{4}$
   1   2   3   1   2   3 *etc.*

2. $\frac{4}{4}$
   1   2   3   4   *etc.*

3. C

Write the counts under the notes and divide the notes into measures.

1. $\frac{3}{4}$

2. $\frac{4}{4}$

3. $\frac{4}{4}$

4. $\frac{3}{4}$

lesson 18

2/4 TIME

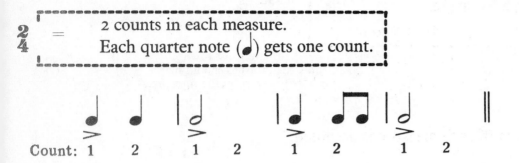

Count: 1   2   1   2   1   2   1   2

In 2/4 time the 1st count of each measure is accented.

● ●

Supply the time signatures for these examples:

Supply the time signatures and add the bar lines for
the following:

lesson 19

NOTE AND REST REVIEW

Add the notes of the proper value to complete these measures:

Example: $\frac{4}{4}$ ♩ | This measure has only one half note, worth two counts. Since it is 4/4 time, the measure should have four counts. Add two counts to complete the measure.

Add the rests of the proper value to complete these measures:

NOTE STEMS

In previous examples you have noticed the note stems
going up on some notes, down on other notes. Here is
the rule that governs the stems:

NOTES ON THE MIDDLE LINE OR HIGHER HAVE STEMS DOWN.

NOTES BELOW THE MIDDLE LINE HAVE STEMS UP.

Add stems to the following notes:

SHARPS

♯ A sharp is a sign which indicates that a note is to be played ½ step higher.

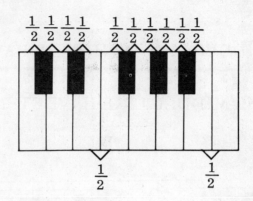

The entire Piano or Organ keyboard is made up of half steps.

 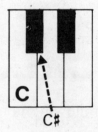

Therefore, a sharp is played on the very next key to the right. (½ step higher).

• •

Write in the name of the sharped note and darken the correct black key:

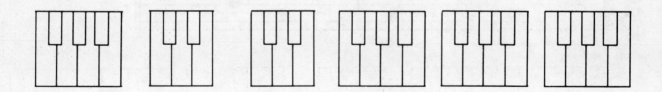

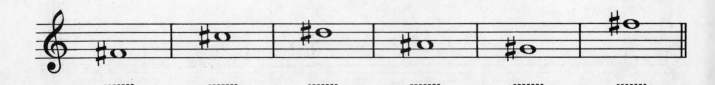

-------   -------   -------   -------   -------   -------

FLATS

♭ A flat is a sign which indicates that a note
is to be played $\frac{1}{2}$ step lower.

A flat is played
on the very next key
to the left. ($\frac{1}{2}$ step lower).

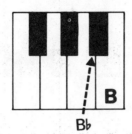

· ·

Write in the name of the flatted or sharped note
and darken the correct black key:

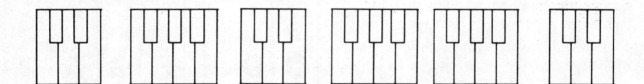

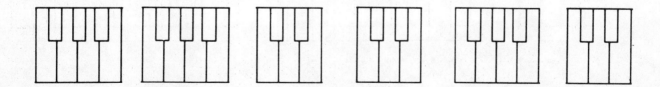

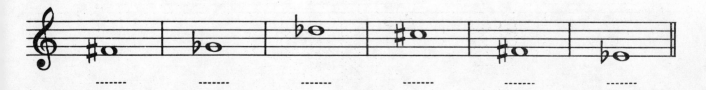

MORE SHARPS AND FLATS

You have already learned that a sharp raises the pitch of a note ½ step, and that a flat lowers the pitch of a note ½ step. By this rule you can see that not all sharps or flats are played on black notes.

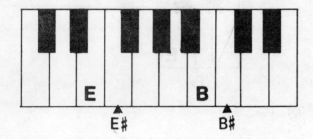
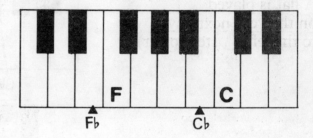

By using all of the note names available, you can see that there are two names for most notes. The more common of the two notes is printed in dark type.

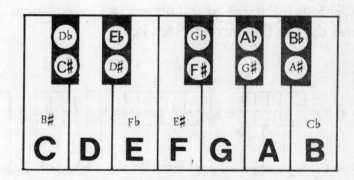

• •

Write in the name of the sharped or flatted note and darken the correct black key:

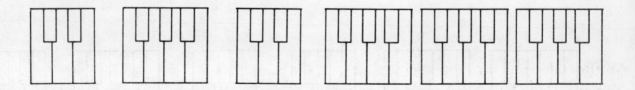

-------   -------   -------   -------   -------   -------

WHOLE STEPS

WHOLE STEP   A whole step is composed of two half steps.

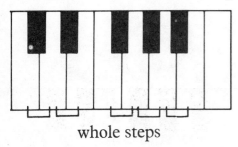

whole steps

Whole steps

In all of these whole steps, we have skipped over the black key in between. Whole steps may also be from black key to white key, white to black, or black to black, just so one key is skipped in between.

whole steps

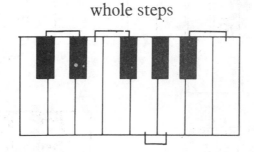

• •

In the following, place a "W" in the blank for a whole step and an "H" for a half step:

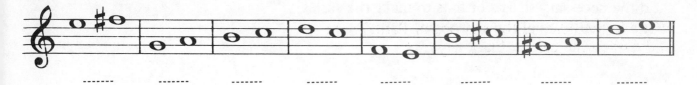

------- ------- ------- ------- ------- ------- ------- -------

In the following, write in a second note, a whole step or a half step higher than the first note, as directed:

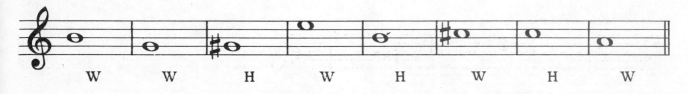

W   W   H   W   H   W   H   W

MAJOR SCALE

A SCALE is a series of notes in succession.
There are several types of scales, each having its own
combination of steps and half steps.

The MAJOR SCALE is the most common scale. It is built
of two whole steps, one half step, three whole steps and one
half step.

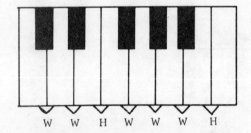
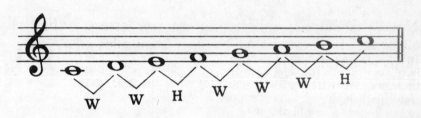

Since this Major Scale pattern was started on C, it is
called the C Major Scale. Major scales may be
started on any note, but must always conform to
the Major Scale pattern of steps and half steps
(W W H W W W H).

● ●

Add the necessary sharps or flats to make the series
of notes conform to the Major Scale pattern:

D Major Scale (use sharps)

F Major Scale (use flats)

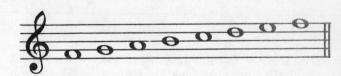

Bb Major Scale (use flats)

G Major Scale (use sharps)

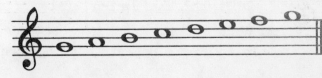

STEP, SKIP OR REPETITION

There are only three ways by which notes may follow
each other—by step, skip or repetition.

STEP

Notes that move to consecutive letters of the alphabet are
said to move by step. That is, they step from C to D,
from F to G, etc. The move by step may be a
whole step or a half step.

SKIP:

Notes that skip an intervening letter or letters of the
alphabet are said to move by skip. Examples of
skips would be C to E, F♯ to A, D to B, etc. Each
of these examples skipped over at least one letter of
the alphabet.

REPETITION

The playing of the same note a second consecutive
time, as C—C, or F♯—F♯.

• •

Tell whether the following examples are step, skip or repetition:

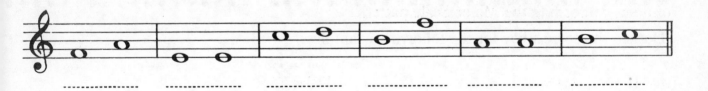

---------------   ---------------   ---------------   ---------------   ---------------   ---------------

Draw a second note in the following examples to complete a step, skip or repeat:

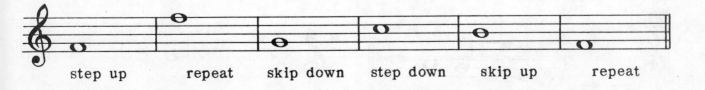

step up   repeat   skip down   step down   skip up   repeat

NATURAL SIGN, ACCIDENTALS

♮ is a Natural Sign. It cancels a sharp or a flat.

Sharps or flats can appear in two different ways:

1. As part of the KEY SIGNATURE at the beginning of a song. As an example, if an F♯ and a C♯ appear in the key signature (key of D) of a song, then all F's and C's in that song are to be played as F sharps and C sharps.

2. To sharp or flat a particular note in the body of a song. This added sharp or flat does not continue on, but ends with the end of the measure in which it appears. A ♯, ♭ or ♮ added in the body of a song is called an ACCIDENTAL.

● ●

Darken the correct key for the following examples:

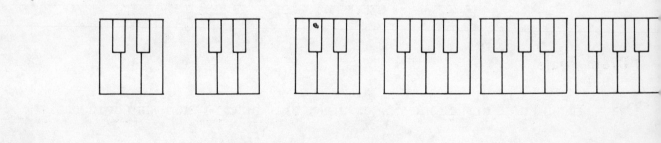

WRITING PRACTICE-RESTS and ACCIDENTALS

Draw Whole Rests

Draw Half Rests

Draw Quarter Rests

Draw Eighth Rests

Draw Sharps

Draw Flats

Draw Naturals

lesson **29**

REVIEW QUIZ

Fill in the blanks:

1. A ......*staff*.... has 5 lines and 4 spaces.

2. 𝄞 is called a .....*Treble*..... clef.

3. ▤ is a .....*Leger*......... line.

4. A .....*¼ ♩*...... note gets one beat in 4/4 Time.

5. A .....*♭*...... lowers a note 1/2 step.

6. ▬ is a .....*W. rest*......

7. ▬ gets ....*2*.... beats in 4/4 Time.

8. Piano music uses the .... staff.

9. A .... gets 2 beats in 3/4 Time.

10. A ♯, ♭ or ♮ in the body of a song is called an ....

11. A sharp .... a note 1/2 step.

12. 𝄾 is a ....

13. Low notes on the piano use the .... staff.

14. The largest note possible in 3/4 Time is ....

15. A .... cancels a sharp or flat.

16. .... is an eighth rest.

PART 2

THEORY NOTEBOOK Complete

lesson 1

REVIEW OF PITCH

THE GREAT STAFF

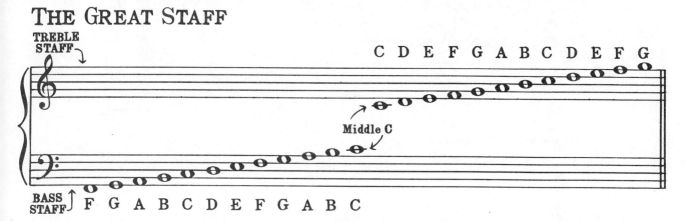

• •

Draw the correct note over each letter name:

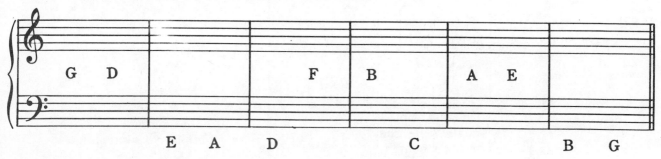

Draw the following notes found on the Great Staff:

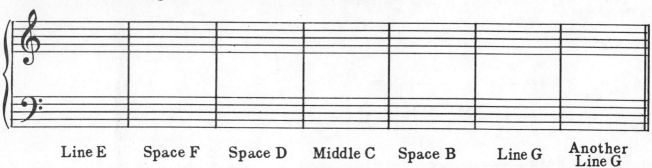

Line E   Space F   Space D   Middle C   Space B   Line G   Another Line G

Fill in the words that these notes spell:

‑‑‑‑‑ ‑‑‑‑‑ ‑‑‑‑‑ ‑‑‑‑‑   ‑‑‑‑‑ ‑‑‑‑‑ ‑‑‑‑‑ ‑‑‑‑‑   ‑‑‑‑‑ ‑‑‑‑‑ ‑‑‑‑‑ ‑‑‑‑‑   ‑‑‑‑‑ ‑‑‑‑‑ ‑‑‑‑‑ ‑‑‑‑‑

REVIEW OF RELATIVE NOTE AND REST VALUES

There are various kinds of NOTES designed to show the duration or time value of a musical sound.

RESTS are symbols indicating a definite duration or time value of silence. Following is a chart showing the relative value of the basic notes and rests.

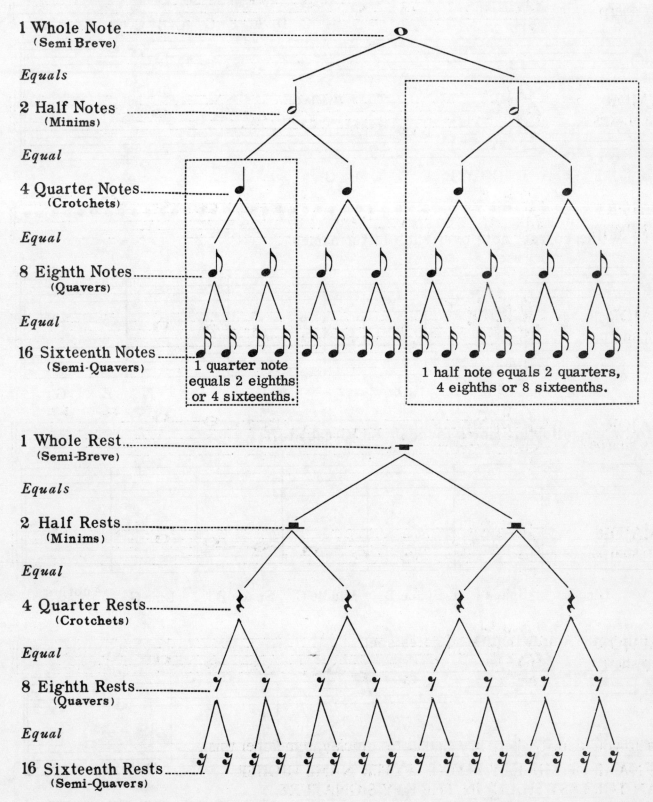

1 Whole Note
(Semi Breve)

Equals

2 Half Notes
(Minims)

Equal

4 Quarter Notes
(Crotchets)

Equal

8 Eighth Notes
(Quavers)

Equal

16 Sixteenth Notes
(Semi-Quavers)

1 quarter note equals 2 eighths or 4 sixteenths.

1 half note equals 2 quarters, 4 eighths or 8 sixteenths.

1 Whole Rest
(Semi-Breve)

Equals

2 Half Rests
(Minims)

Equal

4 Quarter Rests
(Crotchets)

Equal

8 Eighth Rests
(Quavers)

Equal

16 Sixteenth Rests
(Semi-Quavers)

lesson 3

MAJOR SCALES AND KEY SIGNATURES – SHARP KEYS

G MAJOR 1 sharp

D MAJOR 2 sharps

A MAJOR 3 sharps

E MAJOR 4 sharps

B MAJOR 5 sharps

F♯ MAJOR 6 sharps

C♯ MAJOR 7 sharps

To help you identify sharp key signatures quickly, remember this:

THE NAME OF THE KEY IS ONE LETTER NAME HIGHER THAN THE LAST SHARP IN THE KEY SIGNATURE.

MAJOR SCALES AND KEY SIGNATURES –FLAT KEYS

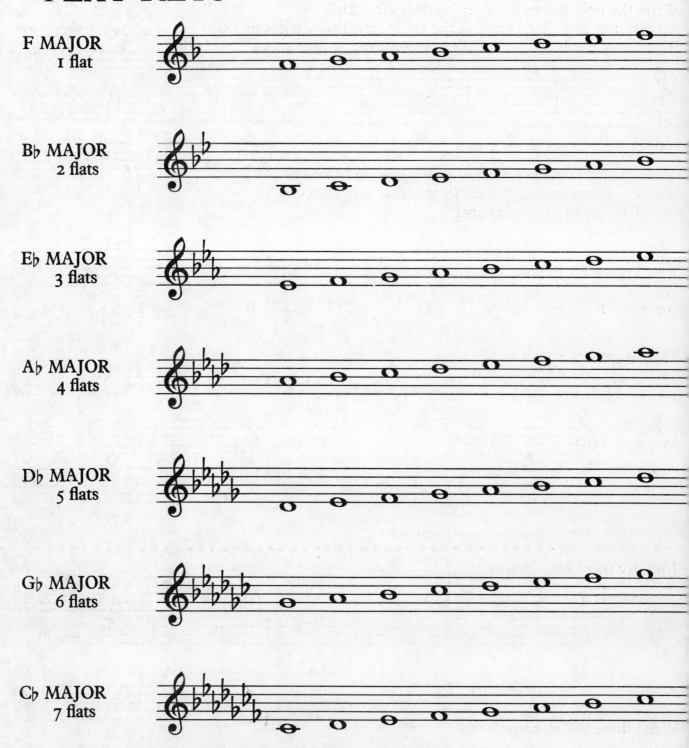

F MAJOR
1 flat

B♭ MAJOR
2 flats

E♭ MAJOR
3 flats

A♭ MAJOR
4 flats

D♭ MAJOR
5 flats

G♭ MAJOR
6 flats

C♭ MAJOR
7 flats

To help you identify flat key signatures quickly, remember this:

1. THE KEY WITH ONE FLAT IS F MAJOR.

2. IN KEYS WITH MORE THAN ONE FLAT, THE NEXT TO THE LAST FLAT IN THE KEY SIGNATURE IS THE NAME OF THE KEY.

REVIEW OF MAJOR KEY SIGNATURES

Write the new sharps in order, as they are added
to each new key, going around the circle of fifths (see lesson 28)
Write only the NEW sharp in each measure:

Key of   G   D   A   E   B   F♯   C♯

Write the new flats in order, as they are added to each
new key, going around the circle of fifths. Write only
the NEW flat in each measure:

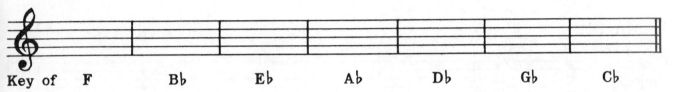

Key of   F   B♭   E♭   A♭   D♭   G♭   C♭

Write these key signatures:

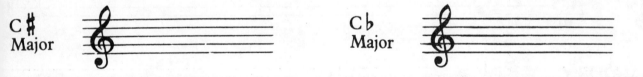

C♯ Major   C♭ Major

You have now written all the sharps and flats in order.

• •

Identify these key signatures:

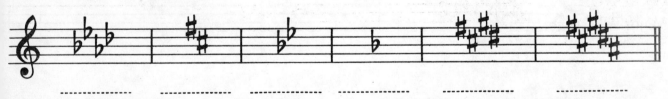

----------   ----------   ----------   ----------   ----------   ----------

Write these key signatures:

G Major   E♭ Major   C Major   D♭ Major   A Major   F Major

MAJOR SCALE REVIEW

Write the following major scales, up and down, using quarter notes.
Add the proper key signature. 1st and last note is given:

KEY IDENTIFICATION THROUGH SPELLING

There are certain sharps or flats which belong
to particular keys.

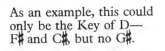 As an example, this could
only be the Key of D—
F♯ and C♯, but no G♯.

Try to identify these keys and then write in the
key signatures:

Key of

Key of

Key of

Key of

Key of

6/8 TIME SIGNATURE

Another variety of time signature has an 8 as the bottom number.

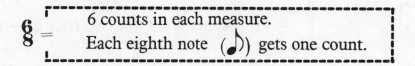

$\frac{6}{8}$ =
- 6 counts in each measure.
- Each eighth note (♪) gets one count.

6/8 time differs from the other time signatures studied in that the 6/8 measure is divided into two parts and has two accents.

1   2   3   4   5   6

Main accent   Small accent

In 6/8 time, or in any other time with an 8 as the bottom number.

♪ = 1 count

♩ = 2 counts

♩. = 3 counts

𝅗𝅥 = 4 counts

𝅗𝅥. = 6 counts

When 6/8 time is fast, you can only feel the two accents in each measure. When it is slow, you can feel all six counts. Since the 6/8 measure is divided into two parts, you can never use a note that extends across the middle of the measure (between beats 3 and 4). The only exception is a note that fills the whole measure, the dotted half note.(𝅗𝅥.)

These measures are all correct. No notes extend across the middle of the measure:

1 2 3 : 4 5 6 | 1 2 3 : 4 5 6 | 1 2 3 : 4 5 6

These measures are NOT correct, because they have notes extending across the middle of the measure:

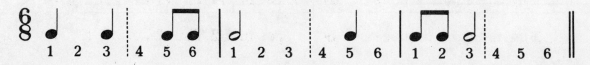

1 2 3 : 4 5 6 | 1 2 3 : 4 5 6 | 1 2 3 : 4 5 6

MORE ABOUT 6/8 TIME

The most important thing to remember about 6/8 Time is how it differs from 3/4 Time. In 6/8 Time, the measure is divided into two parts.

$\frac{6}{8}$ =

In 3/4 Time, the measure is divided into three parts, rather than into two parts.

$\frac{3}{4}$ =

Both 3/4 and 6/8 Time contain a total of six eighth notes per measure, but the arrangement of accents is different. In 6/8 Time, watch for these typical rhythm patterns.

• •

Add the proper Time Signatures. Write the counts under the notes.

Answer these questions:

1. How many beats does [♪♪♪] get in 6/8 Time? ....

2. How many beats does [♪♪♪] get in 3/4 Time? ....

3. How many beats does ♩ get in ¢ Time? ....

4. How many beats does ♩ get in C Time? ....

5. How many beats does ♩ get in 6/8 Time? ....

6. How many beats does ♩ get in ¢ Time? ....

7. How many beats does ♩. get in 3/4 Time? ....

8. How many beats does o get in 2/2 Time? ....

REVIEW OF TIME SIGNATURES

The grouping of counts into measures is indicated by the Time Signature, which appears at the beginning of each song.

The top number of the Time Signature tells how many counts in each measure. The bottom number tells what kind of note is to receive one count.

4/4 = 4 counts in each measure.
Each quarter note (♩) gets one count.

C = Common Time. This sign is often used as a substitute for 4/4 Time.

2/4 = 2 counts in each measure.
Each quarter note (♩) gets one count.

3/4 = 3 counts in each measure.
Each quarter note (♩) gets one count.

6/8 = 6 counts in each measure.
Each eighth note (♪) gets one count.
(or: 2 three-note groups of eighth notes in each measure.)

2/2 = 2 counts in each measure.
Each half note (♩) gets one count.

3/2 = 3 counts in each measure.
Each half note (♩) gets one count.

₵ 2/2 is often called Cut Time, and is designated by this sign: **₵**
The **C** of Common Time is cut in two.   **C** (4/4) becomes **₵** (2/2).

• •

Fill in the blanks:

1. The largest note possible in 3/4 Time is ....

2. **C** means the same as ....

3. In 3/2 Time, the .... note gets three counts.

4. In **₵** Time, the whole note gets .... counts.

5. In 6/8 Time, the .... note gets one count.

6. The most common Time Signs have a .... as the bottom number.

2/2, 3/2 TIME SIGNATURES

Another type of time signature, much less common
than the one with a 4 as the bottom number, is
the type with a 2 as the bottom number.

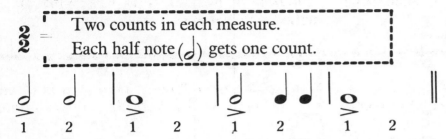

2/2 = Two counts in each measure.
Each half note (♩) gets one count.

```
♩   ♩  |  𝅝  |  ♩  ♩ ♩ |  𝅝  ‖
1   2     1  2    1  2  2    1  2
```

The first count is accented.

3/2 = Three counts in each measure.
Each half note (♩) gets one count.

```
♩   ♩   ♩  | ♩  ♩ ♩ ♩ | 𝅝       ♩ ♩ | 𝅝.  ‖
1   2   3    1  2 3  3    1  2  3    1  2 3
```

The first count is accented.

¢ 2/2 is often called cut time and is designated
by this sign ¢ The C of common time is
cut in two. C (4/4) becomes ¢ (2/2).

• •

Write the counts under the notes and add the bar lines:

TIME SIGNATURE QUIZ

Identify these time signatures, write the counts under the notes and add the bar lines:

Fill in the blanks:

1. ....is the largest note possible in 6/8 time.

2. In 3/2 the.........note gets one count.

3. In.........time there are 6 beats in each measure.

4. The measure is divided in the middle in.........time.

5. ....time and.........time have 3 beats in each measure.

6. The largest note possible in 2/4 time is..........

7. The most common time sign is..........

8. In.........time the eighth note gets one count.

9. The largest note possible in 3/4 time is..........

10. A dotted quarter note is most likely to appear in.........time.

11. The bottom number of a time sign may be........., ...or..........

12. ₵ is called.........time.

TIES

A tie is a curved line connecting two notes of the
same pitch. The first note is played and held for
the combined count of the two notes, without re-striking.

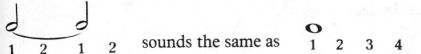

A tie is necessary if you wish to hold a note beyond the bar line.

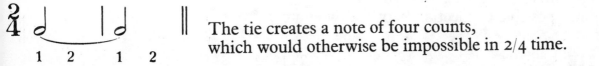

The tie creates a note of four counts,
which would otherwise be impossible in 2/4 time.

• •

Fill in the required notes. Assume all examples to be in 4/4 time:

Tie a half note to
a quarter note.

How many total
beats are there ?.........

Tie a whole note to
a dotted half note.

How many total
beats are there ?.........

Tie a dotted quarter
note to an eighth note.

How many total
beats are there ?.........

Tie a quarter note
to a quarter note.

How many total
beats are there ?.........

SLURS

The same line ⌒‾‾‾ is used for ties or slurs.

The line may be drawn like this ⌒‾‾‾ or like

this ‾‾‾⌣ . They both have the same meaning.

A TIE is a curved line connecting two notes
of the same pitch.

A SLUR connects two or more notes of different
pitch. A slur means to play the notes as
smoothly as possible. (As you can see, the tie
is the smoothest possible connection between two notes).

This is a TIE

This is a SLUR

• •

Indicate whether the following are ties or slurs:

- - - - - - - - - - - - - - - - -

- - - - - - - - - - - - - - - - -

- - - - - - - - - - - - - - - - -

- - - - - - - - - - - - - - - - -

REPEAT SIGN

Sometimes the double bar is used in pairs
to indicate a repeat. The measures within the
repeat sign are played twice. The repeat sign
always has two dots on the inside, facing
the measures to be repeated.

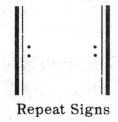

Repeat Signs

is played

• •

Fill in the blanks:

1. ………gets one beat in 2/4 time.

2. ………is the largest note possible in 3/4 time.

3. ♩ ♩ ♩ ♩ ♩ ♩ ♩ 𝅝 ‖ is an example of………time.

4. A double bar is used to indicate the……….

5. ……….is the largest note possible in 2/4 time.

6. What do 2/4, 3/4 and 4/4 have in common?…………………………………………….

7. The top number in a time signature tells how many……….in a……….

8. ………is the largest note possible in 4/4 time.

1ST AND 2ND ENDINGS

Sometimes, when the music repeats itself, 1st and 2nd endings are used, in order to save space.

By using 1st and 2nd endings, the passage can be written like this: Notice that measures ① ② ③ are the same as ⑤ ⑥ ⑦

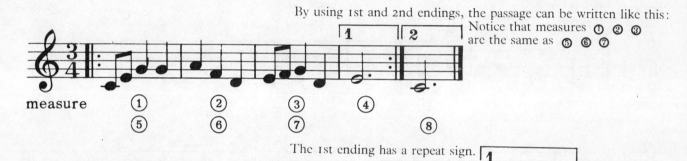

The 1st ending has a repeat sign.

It is called the 1st ending because it is only played the first time through. The second time through, the 1st ending is skipped over, and the 2nd ending is played.

• •

Re-write these examples with 1st and 2nd endings:

CHROMATIC SCALE

In addition to the major scale, which you have already studied,
there are several other types of scales. One of these is
the Chromatic Scale. The chromatic scale pattern is
very simple—it is all half-steps. Every key, black
and white, is played consecutively, in order to play a chromatic
scale. There are 12 different black and white keys.
Scales begin and end on the same letter name, therefore
there are 13 notes in the chromatic scale.

Here is, the chromatic scale
Scale starting on C

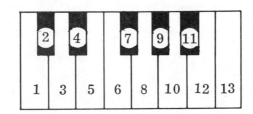

The only confusion concerning chromatic scales is whether to use
sharps of flats for the black notes. The rule is simple:

USE SHARPS GOING UP, USE FLATS GOING DOWN.

A chromatic scale may begin on any note and the rules governing it are always the same.

• •

Add the proper notes, sharps and flats for part of a
chromatic scale, from G up to B and back again:

INTERVALS

An interval is the distance between two notes. The number size
of an interval is figured by counting the total number of
letter names between the two notes inclusively. (Always
count up the alphabet).

C—D   includes only two letters of the alphabet,
        C and D, so the interval is a 2nd.

D—F   includes three letters of the alphabet,
        D, E and F, so the interval is a 3rd.

A—G   includes seven letters of the alphabet, A, B,
        C, D, E, F and G, so the interval is a 7th.

Here are some more examples:

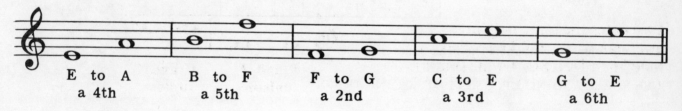

| E to A | B to F | F to G | C to E | G to E |
| a 4th | a 5th | a 2nd | a 3rd | a 6th |

Identify these intervals:

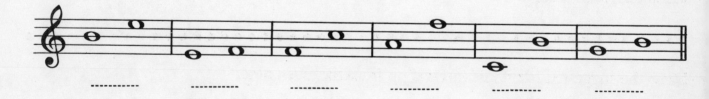

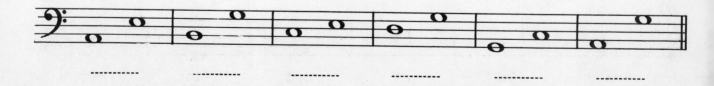

HARMONIC AND MELODIC INTERVALS

An interval which appears in a melody, one note at a time, is called a MELODIC INTERVAL.

Melodic Interval
of a 5th

An interval of two notes, played at the same time, is called a HARMONIC INTERVAL.

Harmonic Interval
of a 5th

During the balance of this book, we will use Harmonic Intervals.

Two intervals which require some explanation are the Unison (1) and the Octave (8th).

Two notes the same only involve one letter name, so would be called a "one" or a UNISON. (one sound)

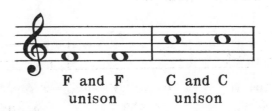

F and F   C and C
unison   unison

Two notes of the same name but of a different pitch are called octaves. (8th)

D to D   F to F
octave   octave

D to D involves eight notes—D, E, F, G, A, B, C and D; therefore it is called an octave.

● ●

Draw the suggested harmonic interval up from the given note:

3rd   5th   octave   6th   unison   2nd

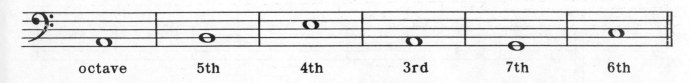

octave   5th   4th   3rd   7th   6th

MAJOR AND MINOR THIRDS

All of the normal chords are built of only
two standard building blocks—the Major 3rd
and the minor 3rd.

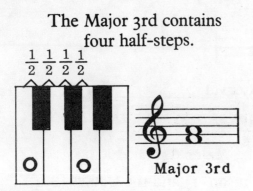

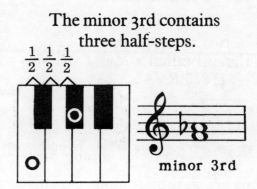

- -

Indicate whether the following are Major 3rd (M3) or minor 3rd (m3):

....

Draw a Major 3rd above each of the following:

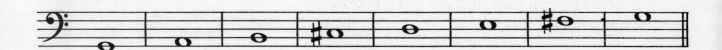

Draw a minor 3rd above each of the following:

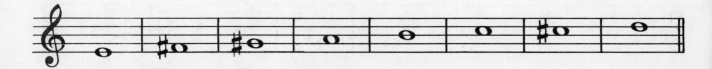

MAJOR AND MINOR TRIADS

A CHORD is a combination of musical tones.

A TRIAD is a three note chord.

A Major Triad is built of a Major 3rd plus a minor 3rd.

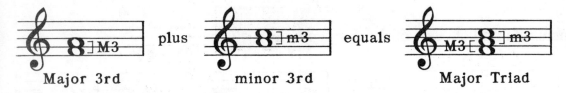

Major 3rd   plus   minor 3rd   equals   Major Triad

Build a Major Triad on each of these given notes:

A minor Triad is built of a minor 3rd plus a Major 3rd.

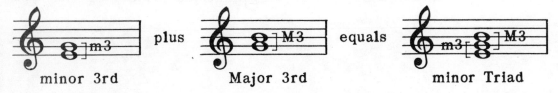

minor 3rd   plus   Major 3rd   equals   minor Triad

Build a minor Triad on each of these given notes:

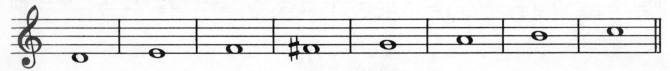

Build the suggested Major (M) or minor (m) triad:

GM   Am   AM   Bm   CM   Dm   EM   Em

AUGMENTED AND DIMINISHED TRIADS

An Augmented Triad is built of a Major 3rd plus a Major 3rd.

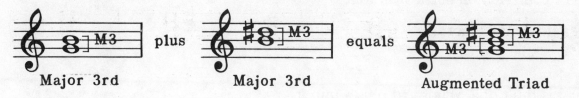

Major 3rd   plus   Major 3rd   equals   Augmented Triad

Build an Augmented Triad on each of these given notes:

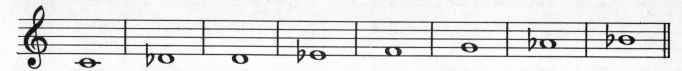

A diminished Triad is built of a minor 3rd plus a minor 3rd.

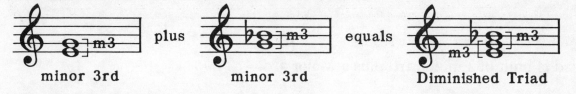

minor 3rd   plus   minor 3rd   equals   Diminished Triad

Build a diminished Triad on each of these given notes:

Build the suggested Augmented (Aug) or diminished (dim) Triad:

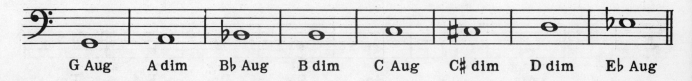

G Aug   A dim   B♭ Aug   B dim   C Aug   C♯ dim   D dim   E♭ Aug

lesson 23

REVIEW OF TRIADS

Identify the following Triads:

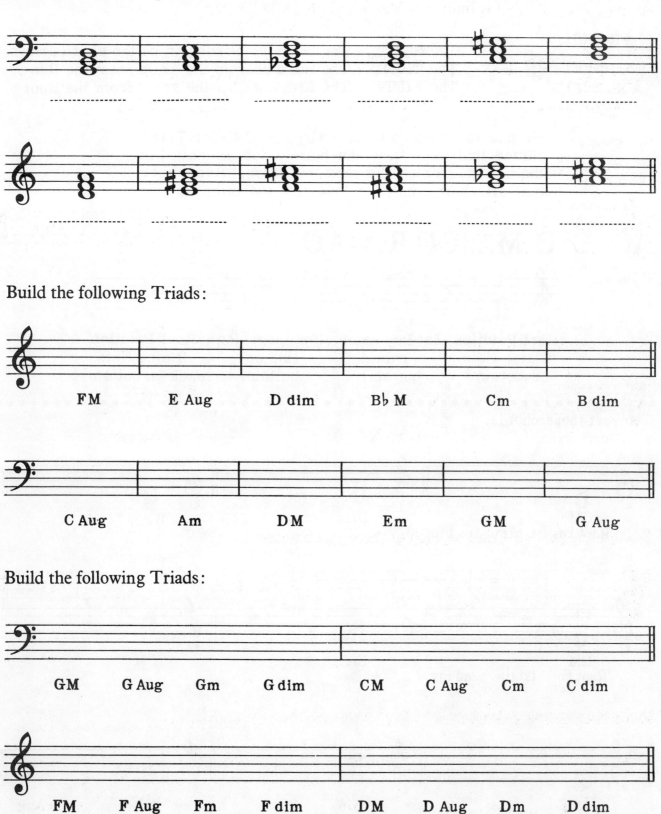

Build the following Triads:

INVERSION OF TRIADS

The word inversion means "turned upside down". To invert a chord you literally do turn it upside down by placing the bottom note on the top.

Fifth (G) — C
Third (E) →
Root (C) →

The three notes of a triad are called:

The ROOT - The name note from which the chord grows.
The THIRD - The third note up the scale from the Root.
The FIFTH - The fifth note up the scale from the Root.

Here is the process of inverting the C Major Triad. Notice that each time the bottom note is moved to the top, it creates the next inversion. Remember that all chords may be inverted and often are.

C MAJOR TRIAD

Root Position (Name Note on bottom)   1st Inversion (3rd on bottom)   2nd Inversion (5th on bottom)   Root Position (Name Note back on bottom)

Invert these chords.

CM — Root Pos. 1st Inv. 2nd Inv.   Dm   B dim

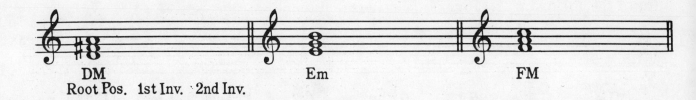

DM — Root Pos. 1st Inv. 2nd Inv.   Em   FM

C aug — Root Pos. 1st Inv. 2nd Inv.   Gdim   EbM

lesson 25

INVERSION QUIZ

Build the following Inversions of Triads:

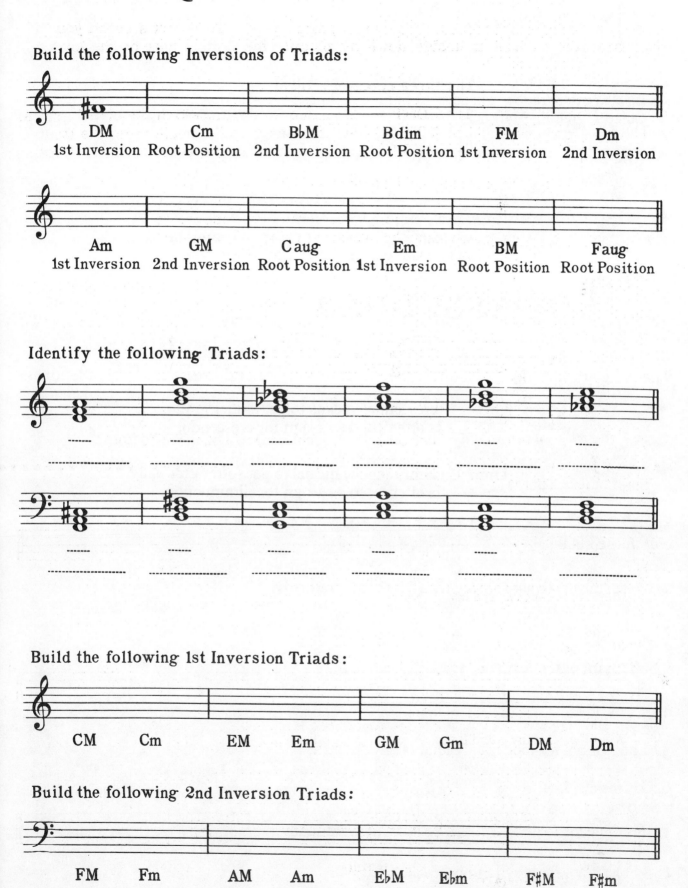

DM	Cm	B♭M	Bdim	FM	Dm
1st Inversion	Root Position	2nd Inversion	Root Position	1st Inversion	2nd Inversion

Am	GM	Caug	Em	BM	Faug
1st Inversion	2nd Inversion	Root Position	1st Inversion	Root Position	Root Position

Identify the following Triads:

Build the following 1st Inversion Triads:

CM	Cm	EM	Em	GM	Gm	DM	Dm

Build the following 2nd Inversion Triads:

FM	Fm	AM	Am	E♭M	E♭m	F♯M	F♯m

DYNAMIC MARKINGS

There are a number of signs, symbols and terms which tell how to interpret the music as to loudness. These are called Dynamic Markings.

SYMBOL	PRONOUNCED (Italian)	MEANING
pp	pianissimo	very soft
p	piano	soft
mp	mezzo piano	moderately soft
mf	mezzo forte	moderately loud
f	forte	loud
ff	fortissimo	very loud

There are other marks which direct the player to increase or decrease the level of loudness.

Cresc. (crescendo) means to get louder gradually.
Is often used as a sign for crescendo.

Dim. (diminuendo) means to get softer gradually.
Is often used as a sign for diminuendo.

● ●

Fill in the blanks:

1. Cresc. means to get...............................gradually.

2. *p* means................................

3. The symbol for very soft is................

4. *f* means................................

5. The symbol for moderately loud is................

6. *m* means................................

7. Dim. means to get...........................gradually.

8. The symbol for very loud is................

TEMPO MARKINGS

There are a number of markings which tell how
to interpret the music as to speed. They are called
Tempo Markings.

slow
{
GRAVE............... slow and solemn
LARGO............... slow and broad
LENTO............... slow
ADAGIO............. leisurely
}

moderate
{
ANDANTE .... moving at a moderate rate
MODERATO........ at a moderate speed
}

fast
{
ALLEGRO........... cheerful, quick
VIVACE.............. very lively
PRESTO............. very fast
PRESTISSIMO..... extremely fast
}

There are other marks which direct the player to
increase or decrease the rate of speed.

rit. (ritard or ritardando) means to get slower gradually.
accel. (accelerando) means to get faster gradually.

● ●

Fill in the blanks:

1. .... means to get slower gradually.

2. Lento means............................

3. .... means slow and solemn.

4. Presto means.............................

5. .... means very lively.

6. Accelerando means............................

7. Moderato means............................

8. A leisurely tempo marking is............................

CIRCLE OF FIFTHS

Keys are related by fifths. As you go to the right on
the keyboard each new key adds a sharp or removes
a flat. As you go to the left each new key adds
a flat or removes a sharp.
C has no sharps or flats. Up a fifth from C is
G, with one sharp. Up a fifth from G is D with
2 sharps, etc. Down a fifth from C is F with
one flat (B♭). Down a fifth from F is B♭ with two
flats, etc.

No ♯ s

C up by 5ths **G**
1♯ - F♯

down by 5ths No ♭ s

F
1♭ - B♭

D
2♯'s - F♯, C♯

B♭
2♭'s - B♭, E♭

**CIRCLE
OF
FIFTHS**

A
3♯'s - F♯, C♯,
G♯

E♭
3♭'s - B♭, E♭, A♭

The three pairs of keys in the boxes at the
bottom of the circle are called enharmonic keys.
They have the same sound, but are spelled
differently.

A♭
4♭'s - B♭, E♭,
A♭, D♭

E
4♯'s - F♯, C♯,
G♯, D♯

B♭, E♭, A♭,
D♭, G♭, A♭

5♭'s

D♭

B♭, E♭, A♭,
D♭, G♭, C♭

6♭'s

G♭

B♭, E♭, A♭,
D♭, G♭, C♭,
F♭ 7♭'s

C♭

C♯
7♯'s
F♯, C♯, G♯,
D♯, A♯, E♯,
B♯

F♯
6♯'s
F♯, C♯, G♯,
D♯, A♯, E♯

B
5♯'s
F♯, C♯, G♯
D♯, A♯

REVIEW QUIZ

lesson **29**

Match the sign or symbol with its correct identification:

ANSWER

1. ------------   a. cut time

2. ------------   b. raises the pitch ½ step

3. **C** ------------   c. cancels a ♯ or ♭

4. ------------   d. treble clef

5. $\frac{6}{8}$ time ------------   e. slur

6. ------------   f. lowers the pitch ½ step

7. ♮ ------------   g. stands for 4/4 time

8. ¢ ------------   h. double bar

9. ♯ ------------   i. bass clef

10. ------------   j. repeat sign

11. ------------   k. accent

12. $\frac{2}{4}$ time ------------   l. the measure is divided in the middle

13. ------------   m. ♩ gets one count

14. > ------------   n. adds half to the value of the note

15. $\frac{3}{2}$ time ------------   o. get softer gradually

16. ♭ ------------   p. ♩ gets one count

lesson 1

LEGER LINES

LEGER LINES, the lines added above or below a staff are added in the same line-space relationship as the rest of the staff.

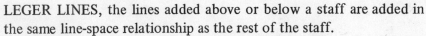

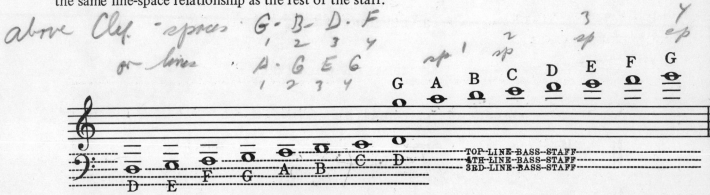

Identify the following Leger Line notes.

32nd AND 64th NOTES AND RESTS

In addition to the basic note and rest values already learned,
there are some less common values.

THIRTY-SECOND NOTE .... ♪ = 𝄿 .... THIRTY-SECOND REST
   (Demisemi quaver)

SIXTY-FOURTH NOTE .... ♪ = 𝄿 .... SIXTY-FOURTH REST
   (Hemidemi semiquaver)

ONE SIXTEENTH NOTE Equals TWO THIRTY-SECOND NOTES ♪ = ♪ + ♪	ONE THIRTY-SECOND NOTE Equals TWO SIXTY-FOURTH NOTES ♪ = ♪ + ♪

• •

In Common Time (♩ = one count) how many counts do each of the following get?

1. 𝅝 ....

2. ♫ ....

3. ♬ ....

4. ♩ + 𝄿 ....

5. 𝅘𝅥𝅰𝅘𝅥𝅰𝅘𝅥𝅰𝅘𝅥𝅰 + ♪ ....

6. 𝄽 + 𝄿 + 𝅘𝅥𝅯 ....

7. ♩. + 𝄿 𝄿 ....

8. 𝅘𝅥𝅰𝅘𝅥𝅰𝅘𝅥𝅰𝅘𝅥𝅰𝅘𝅥𝅰𝅘𝅥𝅰𝅘𝅥𝅰𝅘𝅥𝅰 ....

9. ♬ + 𝅘𝅥𝅯𝅘𝅥𝅯 + 𝄿 ....

10. ▬ ....

Draw the following notes and rests.

1. A 2 count rest ....

2. A 64th rest ....

3. A 1 count note ....

4. A half count rest ....

5. A 32nd note ....

6. 4 notes equalling 1 count ....

7. A 32nd rest ....

8. A half count note ....

9. A 64th note ....

10. A 4 count rest ....

COMPOUND TIME SIGNATURES

COMPOUND METER In certain Time Signatures, the fundamental beat is divided by three instead of being divided by the normal two. This sub-division of the fundamental beat by three is called Compound Meter. For example, 6/8 Time (♪♪♪ ♪♪♪) is actually two counts in the measure, with each count sub-divided by three. 6/8 Time is technically called Compound Duple Meter. Following are two more examples of Compound Meter.

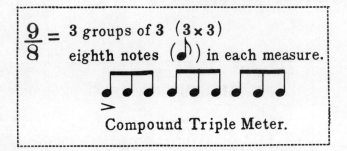

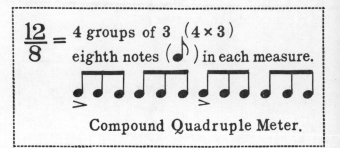

SIMPLE METER   When the fundamental beat is not sub-divided by three the Meter is called Simple Meter. Some examples of Simple Meter that have already been learned are 2/4, 3/4, 4/4, 2/2 and 3/2. A new Simple Meter is 3/8.

$$\frac{3}{8} = \text{3 counts in each measure.}$$
Each eighth note (♪) gets one count.

• •

Supply the Time Signatures for the following.

TRIPLETS

TRIPLET — A Triplet is a group of three equal notes played in the time of one note of the next larger value.

By the use of the Triplet, the beat may be subdivided by three instead of the normal subdivision by two. Not all groups of three eighth notes are Triplets. In order to be a Triplet there must be a slur and a 3 (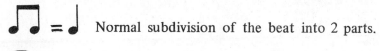) over the notes.

Normal subdivision of the beat into 2 parts.

Triplet subdivision of the beat into 3 parts.

Three eighth notes, not a Triplet, equals a dotted quarter note (1½ beats).

Other note values, in addition to eighth notes may be used to form Triplets, although the eighth note triplet is the most common.

The only requirement of a Triplet is that is be "a group of three equal notes played in the time of one note of the next larger value."

Historically, COMPOUND METER came about through the use of Triplets. The normal subdivision of the beat is into two equal parts. When a composer decided to subdivide the beat into three equal parts, he used the Triplet Sign. In a full piece of music it becomes very awkward to place a Triplet Sign over every beat, measure after measure. Instead, the Time Signatures for Compound Meter were devised.

2/4 Time with each beat subdivided by three became 6/8 Time. 6/8 Time has two beats in each measure, with each beat subdivided by three. When 3/4 Time was played with the beat subdivided by three, it became 9/8 Time. It has three beats in each measure, with each beat subdivided by three, for a total of 9 eighth notes. This same process of subdivision holds true for all other Compound Meter Time Signatures, including 12/8, 6/4 and others.

Following is an example of Compound Duple (3 x 2) Time, written in 2/4 Time with Triplets, and then in 6/8 Time. The sound of both examples is exactly the same. Only the notation is different.

32618

TIME SIGNATURES WITH UNEQUAL DIVISION

In Twentieth Century Music, jazz as well as concert, two Time
Signatures with uneven division of the measure have become popular.
They are 5/4 and 7/4.

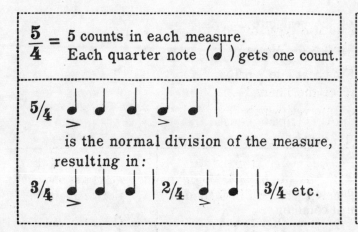

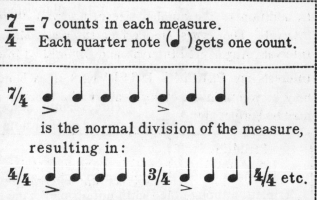

As you have seen, any number can be the top number of a Time Signature.
Since the bottom number of the Time Signature represents kinds of notes,
it must be a 2, 4, 8, or rarely a 16.

• •

Supply the Time Signatures and add the bar lines for the following.

INTERVALS, PERFECT INTERVALS

An INTERVAL is the distance between two notes.

The number size of an interval is figured by counting the total number of letter names, including the bottom and top notes. Always count up the scale.

> The interval of D to G includes four letters of the alphabet — D, E, F and G. Therefore it is a 4th.

In addition to the number size of intervals, there are also types of intervals. The types are Perfect Intervals, Major Intervals, Minor Intervals, Augmented Intervals and Diminished Intervals.

Intervals are PERFECT INTERVALS if each note of the interval may be found in the Major Scale of the other note. Intervals which may be Perfect are:

PRIMES (same note)	4ths (G is found in C Major & C is found in G Major)	5ths (G is found in D Major & D is found in G Major)	OCTAVES (Primes an octave apart)

Seconds, Thirds, Sixths and Sevenths may not be Perfect Intervals.

● ●

Build the following Perfect Intervals above the given notes.

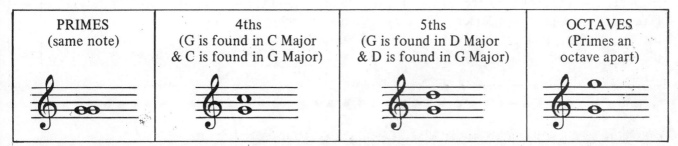

Perf. 5th   Perf. 4th   Perf. Prime   Perf. Octave   Perf. 4th   Perf. 5th

Supply the lower notes for the following Perfect Intervals.

Perf. Octave   Perf. 5th   Perf. 4th   Perf. 4th   Perf. Octave   Perf. 5th

Identify these Perfect Intervals.

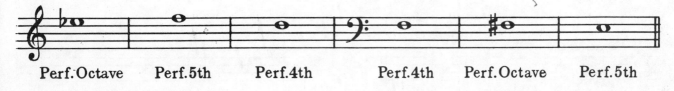

------------ ------------ ------------ ------------ ------------ ------------

MAJOR AND MINOR INTERVALS

An interval is a MAJOR INTERVAL if the upper note may be found in the Major Key of the lower note. Seconds, Thirds, Sixths and Sevenths may be Major Intervals.

Build the following Major Intervals above the given notes.

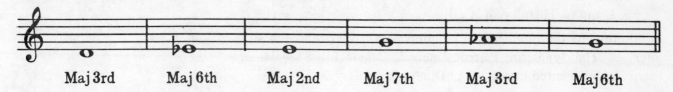

MINOR INTERVALS are one half step smaller than the Major Intervals with the same number size. C to E is a Major 3rd, but C to E flat or C sharp to E is a Minor 3rd. You may make the interval a half step smaller, thus changing it from Major to Minor by lowering the top note or by raising the bottom note.

• •

Change these intervals from Major to Minor by Lowering the top note.

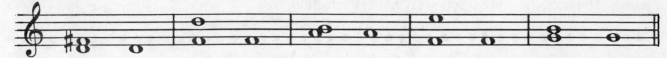

Change these intervals from Major to Minor by raising the bottom note.

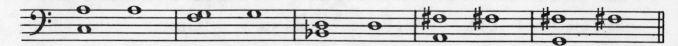

Change these intervals from Minor to Major.

Tell whether the following intervals are Major, Minor or Perfect.

---------- ---------- ---------- ---------- ---------- ---------- ---------- ----------

lesson 8

AUGMENTED AND DIMINISHED INTERVALS

The following chart shows the progression of intervals from Diminished to Augmented. Notice these facts:

1. A Major Interval made 1/2 step smaller becomes a Minor Interval.
2. A Minor Interval made 1/2 step larger becomes a Major Interval.
3. A Minor of Perfect Interval made 1/2 step smaller becomes a Diminished Interval.
4. A Major or Perfect Interval made 1/2 step larger becomes an Augmented Interval.

	← Smaller		Larger →	
2nds, 3rds, 6ths, 7ths	Diminished	Minor	Major	Augmented
Primes, 4ths, 5ths, Octaves	Diminished	Perfect		Augmented

• •

Change these intervals to Diminished Intervals by adding accidentals.

Change these intervals to Augmented Intervals by adding accidentals.

Build the following intervals above the given notes.

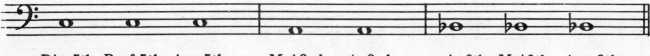

Dim 5th   Perf. 5th   Aug 5th   Maj 3rd   min 3rd   min 6th   Maj 6th   Aug 6th

INVERSION OF INTERVALS

Intervals are inverted in the same manner that chords are inverted. The bottom note is moved to the top by raising it an octave. However, when intervals are inverted they become opposite, as if shown in a mirror. When intervals are inverted, both the number size and the type change.

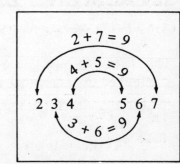

The NUMBER SIZE of an interval and its inversion always add up to 9. Therefore, a 2nd inverted becomes a 7th (2 + 7 = 9), a 3rd inverted becomes a 6th (3 + 6 = 9), a 4th inverted becomes a 5th (4 + 5 = 9), etc.

2nd becomes 7th   3rd becomes 6th   4th becomes 5th

The TYPE OF INTERVAL becomes opposite when inverted. Major becomes Minor, Minor becomes Major, Augmented becomes Diminished, Diminished becomes Augmented, but Perfect remains Perfect.

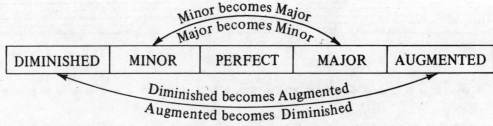

Putting these two rules together, we find that a Minor 2nd inverted becomes a Major 7th. Minor becomes Major and 2nd becomes 7th. (2 + 7 = 9) A Diminished 3rd inverted becomes an Augmented 6th. Diminished becomes Augmented and 3rd becomes 6th. (3 + 6 = 9) A Perfect 5th inverted becomes a Perfect 4th. Perfect stays Perfect and 5th becomes 4th. (5 + 4 = 9)

● ●

Supply these answers concerning inversions of intervals.

1. Augmented is the opposite of ....

2. Major is the opposite of ....

3. Perfect inverted is..

4. An Augmented 4th inverted becomes a ....

5. A Minor 3rd inverted becomes a...

6. A Diminished 7th inverted becomes an ....

7. A Major 6th inverted becomes a ....

lesson 10

INTERVAL CHART AND QUIZ

CHART OF COMMON INTERVALS

* ENHARMONIC: Same sound but different notation.

● ●

Identify these intervals as to number and type.

Build the following intervals:

Dim 7th   Maj 2nd   Aug 4th   Maj 3rd   Perf.4th   Maj 6th

Dim 5th   Maj 7th   Min 3rd   Min 2nd   Min 6th   Min 7th

TRIAD REVIEW

A Triad is a three note chord. When it is in Root Position (with its name note on the bottom) it consists of alternate letter names — A C E, B D F, etc. Also, when in Root Position, the notes of the triad are either on three consecutive lines or three consecutive spaces. Triads in Root Position are built of only two types of intervals — the Major 3rd (with 4 half steps) and the Minor 3rd (with 3 half steps). In Root Position, the names of the three notes of any triad are Root, 3rd and 5th.

A Major Triad is built of a Major 3rd plus a minor 3rd.

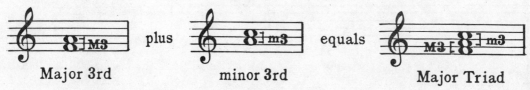

A minor Triad is built of a minor 3rd plus a Major 3rd

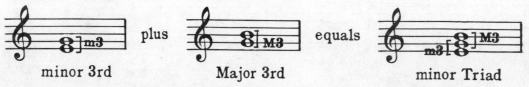

An Augmented Triad is built of a Major 3rd plus a Major 3rd.

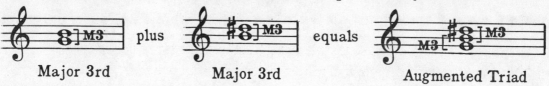

A diminished Triad is built of a minor 3rd plus a minor 3rd.

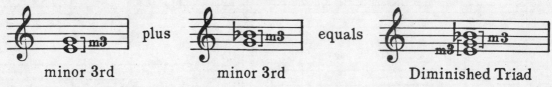

• •

Fill in the blanks, indicating type of 3rd and type of Triad.

1. _____ 3rd + _____ 3rd = _____ Triad   2. _____ 3rd + _____ 3rd = _____ Triad

3. _____ 3rd + _____ 3rd = _____ Triad   4. _____ 3rd + _____ 3rd = _____ Triad

CHANGING TRIADS

To change a Major Triad into a Minor Triad, lower the middle note (the 3rd) ½ step. This changes the formula of the Major Triad — Major 3rd plus minor 3rd, into the formula of the Minor Triad — minor 3rd plus Major 3rd.

Change the following chords from Major to minor.

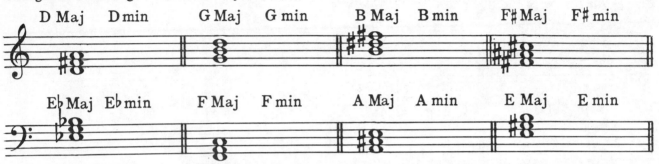

To change a Minor Triad into a Major Triad, raise the middle note (the 3rd) ½ step. This changes the formula of the Minor Triad — minor 3rd plus Major 3rd, into the formula of the Major Triad — Major 3rd plus minor 3rd.

Change the following chords from minor to Major.

To change a Major Triad into an Augmented Triad, raise the top note (the 5th) ½ step. This changes the formula of the Major Triad — Major 3rd plus minor 3rd, into the formula of the Augmented Triad — Major 3rd plus Major 3rd.

Change the following chords from Major to Augmented.

lesson 13

CHANGING MORE TRIADS

To change an Augmented Triad into a Major Triad, lower the top note (the 5th) ½ step. This changes the formula of the Augmented Triad – Major 3rd plus Major 3rd, into the formula of the Major Triad – Major 3rd plus minor 3rd.

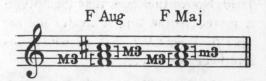

Change the following chords from Augmented to Major.

To change a Minor Triad into a Diminished Triad, lower the top note (the 5th) ½ step. This changes the formula of the Minor Triad – minor 3rd plus Major 3rd, into the formula of the Diminished Triad – minor 3rd plus minor 3rd.

Change the following chords from minor to diminished.

To change a Diminished Triad into a Minor Triad, raise the top note (the 5th) ½ step. This changes the formula of the Diminished Triad – minor 3rd plus minor 3rd, into the formula of the Minor Triad – minor 3rd plus Major 3rd.

Change the following chords from diminished to minor.

INVERSION AND TRIAD QUIZ

Here is the process of inverting the C Major Triad. Notice that each time the bottom note is moved to the top, it creates the next inversion. Remember that all chords may be inverted and often are.

C MAJOR TRIAD

| Root Position (Name Note on bottom) | 1st Inversion (3rd on bottom) | 2nd Inversion (5th on bottom) | Root Position (Name Note back on bottom) |

Place the following chords in Root Position and supply their proper names.

C min

Invert these triads.

F Maj   G min   A Maj

Root Pos. 1st Inv. 2nd Inv.

D min   E Maj   C Aug

Identify the following triads as to name and inversion.

G min
1st Inversion

DOMINANT 7th AND MAJOR 7th CHORDS

A SEVENTH CHORD is a four note chord. It gets its name from the interval between the top and bottom notes.

The most common seventh chord is the DOMINANT SEVENTH chord. A Dominant Seventh chord is built of a Major 3rd plus a minor 3rd plus a minor 3rd. (You have already learned that a Major 3rd plus a minor 3rd is a Major Triad, so a Dominant Seventh is a Major Triad plus a minor 3rd.)

Major 3rd   plus   minor 3rd   plus   minor 3rd   equals   Dominant 7th

----

Another seventh chord built on the Major Triad is the MAJOR SEVENTH chord. It is built of a Major 3rd plus a minor 3rd plus a Major 3rd.

Major 3rd   plus   minor 3rd   plus   Major 3rd   equals   Major 7th

• •

Identify these seventh chords:

--------   --------   --------   --------   --------   --------

Build the suggested seventh chords:

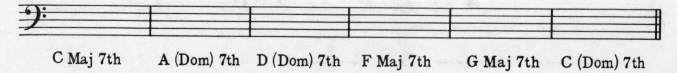

C Maj 7th   A (Dom) 7th   D (Dom) 7th   F Maj 7th   G Maj 7th   C (Dom) 7th

MINOR 7th AND DIMINISHED 7th CHORDS

Another common seventh chord is the MINOR SEVENTH chord. A Minor Seventh chord is built of a minor 3rd plus a Major 3rd plus a minor 3rd. (You have already learned that a minor 3rd plus a Major 3rd is a Minor Triad, so a Minor Seventh is a Minor Triad plus a minor 3rd.)

| minor 3rd | Major 3rd | minor 3rd | minor 7th |

The DIMINISHED SEVENTH Chord is built on the Diminished Triad. It is built of a minor 3rd plus a minor 3rd plus a minor 3rd.

| minor 3rd | minor 3rd | minor 3rd | Diminished 7th |

The four most important types of Seventh Chords:

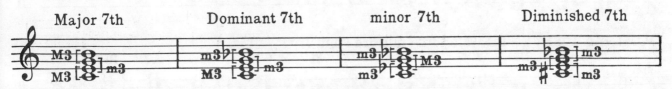

| Major 7th | Dominant 7th | minor 7th | Diminished 7th |

• •

Identify these Seventh Chords:

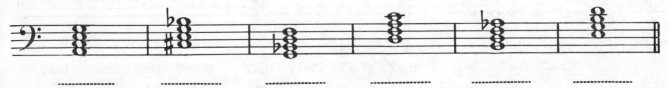

Build the suggested Seventh Chords:

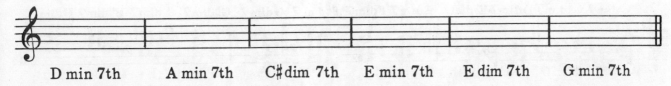

D min 7th A min 7th C#dim 7th E min 7th E dim 7th G min 7th

TABLE OF ROOT POSITION CHORDS

Spelling of some chords has been altered to make reading easier

GENERAL CHORD QUIZ

Fill in the blanks:

1. How many notes are there in a Triad? ....

2. The names of the notes in a Triad are the ...., ... and ....

3. The four types of Triads are ...., ..., ... and ....

4. The formula for the Diminished Triad is .... plus ....

5. To convert a Major Triad to Augmented .... the ....

6. The position of a chord with the name note on the bottom is the .... position.

7. A Major Triad plus a minor 3rd equals a ....

8. The formula for the Minor Seventh is .... plus .... plus ....

Identify the following chords:

Build the suggested chords:

| G min | Eb Aug | F Maj | F# dim 7th | C Maj 7th | E min |
| | | 1st Inversion | | | 2nd Inversion |

| A Maj | C# dim 7th | B min | E min 7th | F# dim | D (Dom) 7th |
| 2nd Inversion | | 1st Inversion | | | |

REVIEW OF MAJOR SCALES AND KEYS

The Major Scale formula is step, step, half step, step, step, step, half
step. Using this formula, build Major Scales starting on the following
notes. Use added sharps or flats.

If necessary, review Major Key signatures, using previous books or
Lesson 20 of this book, Then, answer the following questions.
Remember, there are certain sharps and flats that belong to parti-
cular keys. Each of the following can only be an example of one
Major Key. Identify that key.

Identify these Key Signatures:

Write these Key Signatures

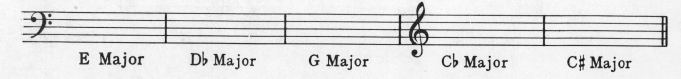

E Major   Db Major   G Major   Cb Major   C# Major

RELATIVE MAJOR AND MINOR KEY CHART

The Major and Minor Keys with the same Key Signature are said to be Relative Major and Minor Keys. The Relative Minor Key is a minor 3rd (three half-steps) lower than the Major Key with the same Key Signature. Example: D Minor is the Relative Minor Key to F Major. D is a minor third lower than F. Both keys have the Key Signature of one flat — B flat.

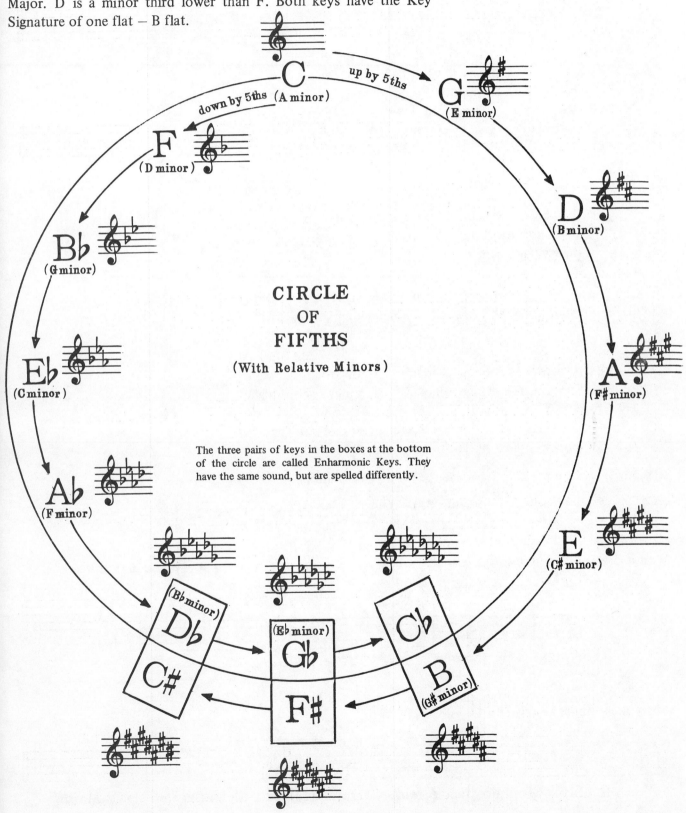

CIRCLE
OF
FIFTHS

(With Relative Minors)

The three pairs of keys in the boxes at the bottom of the circle are called Enharmonic Keys. They have the same sound, but are spelled differently.

RELATIVE MAJOR AND MINOR KEY SIGNATURES

The concept of Relative Major — Minor Keys is useful to help the student find the Minor Key Signatures without learning a whole new set of signatures all at once. He can do it by relating to the already learned Major Key Signatures.

Example 1. What is this Minor Key?

We know that this is the Key Signature for the Key of G Major. To find the Relative Minor, count down a minor 3rd (3 half steps). A minor 3rd down from G is E. Therefore, this is the Key Signature of the Key of E Minor.

Example 2. What is this Minor Key?

This is the Key Signature for the Key of E Flat Major. C is a minor 3rd below E flat. Therefore, this is the Key Signature of the Key of C Minor.

The proper sharps or flats for a given Minor Key Signature can also be found by relating to the already learned Major Key Signatures.

Example 1. What is the Key Signature for the Key of D Minor?

The Relative Major Key is found a minor 3rd (3 half steps) higher than its Relative Minor Key. F is a minor 3rd higher than D. We know that F Major has a Key Signature of one flat — B flat. Therefore, the Key Signature of the Key of D Minor is one flat — B flat.

Example 2. What is the Key Signature for the Key of B Minor?

D is a minor 3rd up from B. D Major has two sharps — F sharp and C sharp. Therefore, the Key Signature for the Key of B Minor is two sharps — F sharp and C sharp.

● ●

Identify the following minor key signatures:

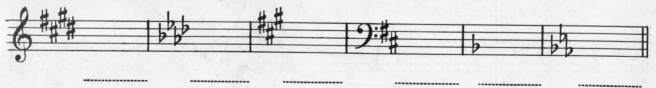

-------------   -------------   -------------   -------------   -------------   -------------

Supply these minor key signatures:

G minor   F# minor   A minor   D minor   C minor   E minor

MINOR SCALES

There are three types of Minor Scales.

1. NATURAL MINOR — This is an old scale, derived from the Gregorian Modes. This scale follows the Minor Key Signature, without any alteration.

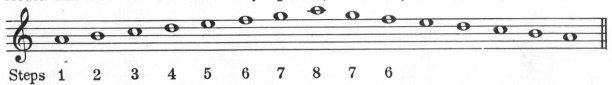

Steps 1   2   3   4   5   6   7   8   7   6

2. HARMONIC MINOR — This is the most commonly used Minor Scale, designed to be used where there is harmony. It raises the 7th scale step.

Steps 1   2   3   4   5   6   7   8   7   6

3. MELODIC MINOR — This form of the Minor Scale was used primarily in the vocal music of the 17th and 18th centuries. Singers found the interval between the 6th and 7th scale steps of the Harmonic Minor Scale difficult to sing, so they raised the 6th scale step, in addition to the 7th, but only going up the scale. Going down the scale they used the Natural Minor form.

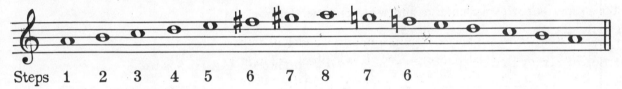

Steps 1   2   3   4   5   6   7   8   7   6

To help you determine which form of Minor Scale is being used, look for the following:

1. Raised 7th scale step — HARMONIC MINOR.

2. Raised 6th and 7th scale steps, going up only — MELODIC MINOR.

3. No alterations of 6th or 7th scale steps — NATURAL MINOR.

● ●

Identify the form of Minor Scale used in each of the following:

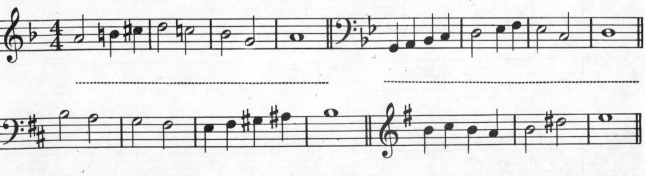

HARMONIC MINOR SCALE

The scale formula for the Harmonic Minor Scale is step, half step, step, step, half step, step and a half, half step. (1 − ½ − 1 − 1 − ½ − 1½ − − ½) Notice the large interval of 1½ steps (3 half steps), between the 6th and 7th scale steps. This is the unique characteristic of the Harmonic form of the Minor Scale.

Practice building Harmonic Minor Scales by adding sharps and flats to conform to the scale formula. Don't worry about the key signature.

Supply the proper Minor Key Signature and write out the Harmonic Minor Scales requested.

C Harmonic Minor Scale   F♯ Harmonic Minor Scale

B Harmonic Minor Scale   A Harmonic Minor Scale

Harmonic Minor Scales can also be formed by altering the Major Scale with the same letter name. To Convert a Major Scale to a Harmonic Minor Scale, lower the 3rd and 6th scale steps of the Major Scale. In the following scales, convert Major to Harmonic Minor by lowering the 3rd and 6th. Compare your results with the scales you have just written.

NATURAL MINOR SCALE

The Natural Minor Scale is sometimes called the Modal Minor, in reference to its origin as one of the Gregorian Modes. The Natural Minor Scale uses the Key Signature without alteration. It might help you to think of the Natural Minor Scale as a scale starting on the 6th step of its Relative Major Scale, without any alteration.

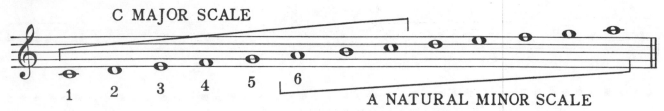

Build the following Natural Minor Scales through the use of the Relative Major Key Signatures. Remember, the Natural Minor Scale starts on the 6th step of its Relative Major Scale.

D NATURAL MINOR SCALE   **G NATURAL MINOR SCALE**

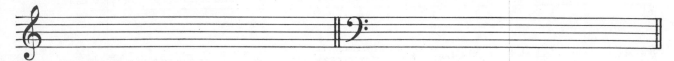

Natural Minor Scales can also be formed by altering the Major Scale with the same letter name. To convert a Major Scale to a Natural Minor Scale, lower the 3rd, 6th and 7th scale steps of the Major Scale. In the following scales, lower the 3rd, 6th and 7th scale steps to convert the Major Scale to a Natural Minor Scale.

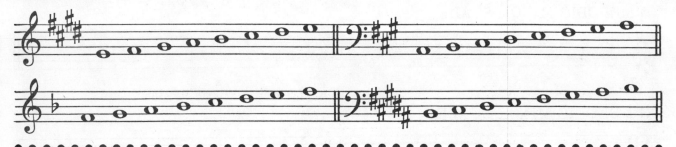

Now write out the same scales as in the example above, but write them out with the proper Key Signatures instead of using accidentals. (Here is another helpful hint: A Major Key has 3 more sharps or 3 less flats than the Minor Key with the same letter name. A Major has 3 sharps. A Minor has no sharps. B Flat Major has 2 flats, B Flat Minor has 5 flats.)

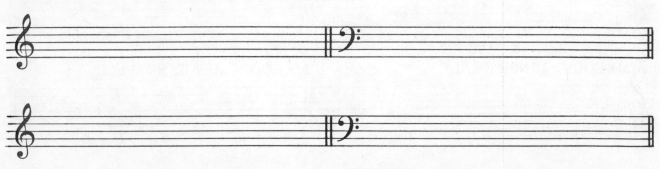

MELODIC MINOR SCALE

The Melodic Minor Scale was developed to make the singing of minor melodies easier. To avoid the difficult augmented 2nd between the 6th and 7th steps of the scale, the 6th and 7th are both raised going up the scale. The Natural Minor form is used going down the scale.

A MELODIC MINOR SCALE

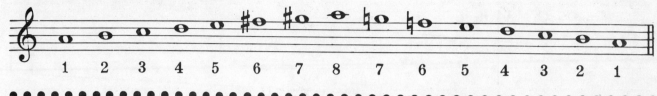

1   2   3   4   5   6   7   8   7   6   5   4   3   2   1

• •

Write the following Melodic Minor Scale, up and back. The proper Key Signatures are supplied for you.

C MELODIC MINOR SCALE

F♯ MELODIC MINOR SCALE

Write the following Melodic Minor Scales up and back. Supply the proper Key Signatures.

E MELODIC MINOR SCALE

G MELODIC MINOR SCALE

Write the top portion of these Melodic Minor Scales. (Supply steps 5, 6, 7, 8, 7, 6, 5.)

D MELODIC MINOR SCALE   F MELODIC MINOR SCALE

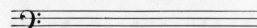

5   6   7   8   7   6   5   5   6   7   8   7   6   5

A MELODIC MINOR SCALE   B MELODIC MINOR SCALE

5   6   7   8   7   6   5   5   6   7   8   7   6   5

GENERAL SCALE QUIZ

Identify the following scales as to letter name and type of scale. If
the scale is a Minor Scale, tell which form of minor is used.

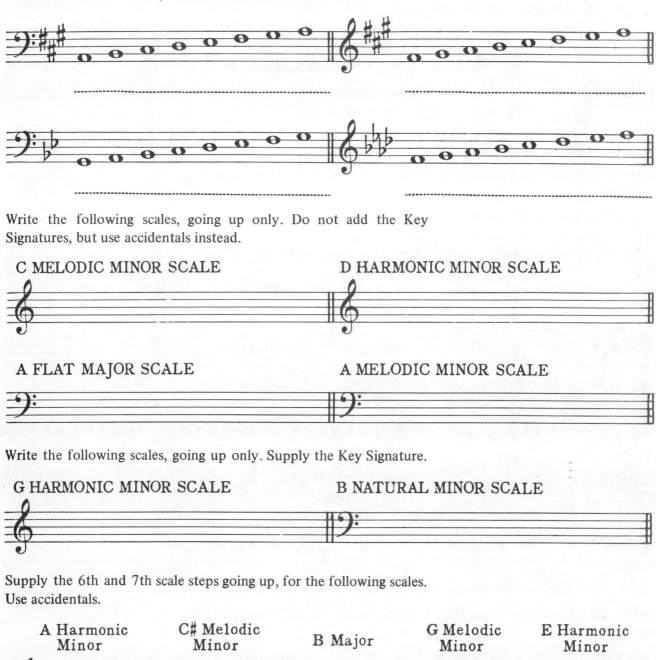

Write the following scales, going up only. Do not add the Key
Signatures, but use accidentals instead.

C MELODIC MINOR SCALE   D HARMONIC MINOR SCALE

A FLAT MAJOR SCALE   A MELODIC MINOR SCALE

Write the following scales, going up only. Supply the Key Signature.

G HARMONIC MINOR SCALE   B NATURAL MINOR SCALE

Supply the 6th and 7th scale steps going up, for the following scales.
Use accidentals.

A Harmonic   C# Melodic   G Melodic   E Harmonic
Minor   Minor   B Major   Minor   Minor

Which scale is each of the following from?

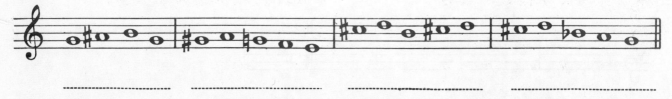

D.C., D.S., CODA AND FINE

There are several signs that are used to direct the player to skip backward or forward through a piece of music. These signs are used to avoid writing out long repeated passages. Some of these signs already discussed are:

THE REPEAT SIGN ‖: :‖ This directs the player to play all music between these two signs twice.

1st and 2nd ENDINGS These direct a player to repeat a section, but to take a different ending the second time.

‖1.   ‖2.

:‖

Some additional signs frequently used are:

D.C. (Da Capo) – Repeat from the beginning.
D.S. (Dal Segno) – Repeat from the sign. (𝄋)
FINE – The end.
D.C. al FINE (Da Capo al Fine) – Repeat from the beginning to the end. (Fine sign)
D.S. al FINE (Dal Segno al Fine) – Repeat from the sign (𝄋) to the end. (Fine sign)
CODA – A section at the end of a piece.
D.C. al ⊕ CODA – Repeat from the beginning to the Coda Sign (⊕) and then skip to the Coda.
D.S. al ⊕ CODA – Repeat from the Sign (𝄋) to the Coda Sign (⊕) and then skip to the Coda.

● ●

Fill in the blanks:

1. .... means the end.

2. A Coda appears at the .... of a piece.

3. .... is a Coda sign.

4. D.C. means to repeat from the ....

Write out this example with 1st and 2nd endings.

lesson 28

SIGNS AND SYMBOLS

There are many signs and symbols used in musical notation. In addition to the notes and rests, there are many signs which tell you how to play the notes.

FERMATA (Hold) — Hold the note longer than the normal value.

Example: A whole note with a fermata, at the end of a piece, might be held for 6 beats instead of the normal 4 beats.

8ve......... **OCTAVE SIGN** — This sign directs a player to play the notes below the dotted line one octave higher. It is usually used to avoid writing hard to read leger lines.

Example: If an Octave Sign were above an F in the 1st space of the treble clef, you would play the F on the top line of the treble clef instead.

STACCATO — The little dot above or below a note it the sign of staccato. The dot directs the performer to play the note very short, detached from all other notes.

ACCENT — Give added emphasis to the note by playing it louder.

SLUR — This curved line (slur) is the sign of Legato. The slur directs the performer to connect the notes under it as smoothly as possible. It is the opposite of staccato.

• •

Match the sign or symbol with its correct identification.

ANSWER

1. ♮ ....   a. Play short, detached
2. *Fine* ....   b. Cancels a sharp or flat
3. ....   c. Raises the pitch of a note ½ step
4. ....   d. Hold longer than normal value
5. ....   e. Adds half to the value of a note
6. ....   f. Time signature
7. ....   g. The end
8. ....   h. Give added emphasis

REVIEW QUIZ

Match the item on the left with the best descriptive phrase on the right.

ANSWER

1. Augmented	....	a. Repeat from the beginning.
2. Harmonic Minor Scale	....	b. The Root is on the bottom.
3. Relatives	....	c. Minor 7th chord.
4. 2nd Inversion	....	d. Interval with 3 half steps.
5. 4/4	....	e. Major Triad.
6. Major—Major	....	f. Major and Minor Keys with same Signature.
7. Major—minor—minor	....	g. Compound meter.
8. Minor 3rd	....	h. Made smaller.
9. Natural Minor Scale	....	i. Interval with 4 half steps.
10. D.S.	....	j. The 5th is on the bottom.
11. 9/8	....	k. Augmented Triad.
12. Major—minor—Major	....	l. Raises 6th and 7th steps going up only.
13. Root Position	....	m. The Sign.
14. D.C.	....	n. Dominant 7th chord.
15. Diminished	....	o. Simple meter.
16. minor—minor	....	p. Has 1½ steps between 6th and 7th scale steps.
17. Melodic Minor Scale	....	q. Major 7th chord.
18. minor—Major—minor	....	r. Repeat from the sign.
19. Major 3rd	....	s. Follows Key Signature without alteration.
20. Fine	....	t. Diminished Triad.
21. ⌢	....	u. Minor Triad.
22. minor-Major	....	v. Diminished 7th Chord.
23. minor-minor-minor	....	w. The 3rd is on the bottom.
24. 1st Inversion	....	x. Made larger.
25. Major-minor	....	y. The end.
26. 𝄋	....	z. Hold longer than normal value.

THEORY NOTEBOOK Complete

ANSWER SHEET

Lesson 1 – H, L, L, S, L, H, S, H, H, S

Lesson 2 – B, D, G, F, D, B, E, G

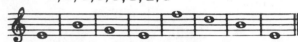

Lesson 3 – F, E, C, E, A, F, C, A

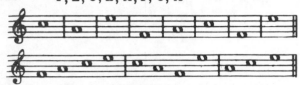

Lesson 4 – D, F, F, G, B, C, A, B
E, G, E, A, D, F, B, E

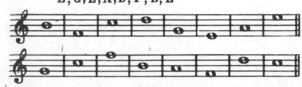

Lesson 5 – B, A, F, D, G, F, A, B

Lesson 6 – A, E, G, E, A, C, G, C

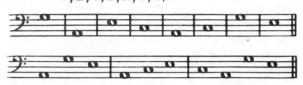

Lesson 7 – E, G, G, E, A, F, C, F, E, A, G, C

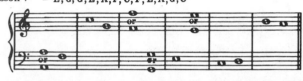

Lesson 9 – BAD/ CAB/ DEAF/ DAD (There is more than one answer to this one)

B A G G A G E   B E G   C A G E   F A D E

Lesson 10

Lesson 11

1. Quarter note,   2. Whole rest,   3. Eighth rest,
4. Half note,   5. Eight note,   6. Whole note,
7. Quarter rest,   8. Half rest.

Lesson 13

2, 4, 1, ½, 1, 2, 1, 2, 4, ½

1. ♩, 2. ⁊, 3. ♪, 4. 𝄽, 5. 𝅝, 6. ▬, 7. ♪, 8. ▬

Lesson 15

3, 1½, 3, 1½, 4, 4, 1½, 6, 3½, 4.

Lesson 17

Lesson 18 – 1, 4/4, 2, 3/4, 3, 2/4, 4, 3/4

ANSWER SHEET

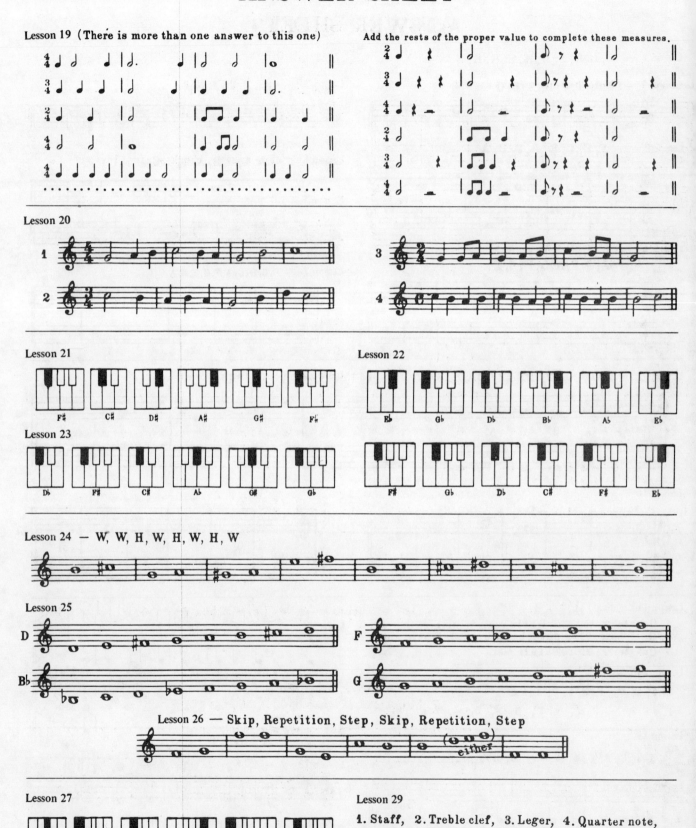

Lesson 19 (There is more than one answer to this one)

Add the rests of the proper value to complete these measures.

Lesson 20

Lesson 21

F# C# D# A# G# F#

Lesson 22

Eb Gb Db Bb Ab Eb

Lesson 23

Db F# C# Ab G# Gb

F# Gb Db C# F# Eb

Lesson 24 — W, W, H, W, H, W, H, W

Lesson 25

D
Bb
F
G

Lesson 26 — Skip, Repetition, Step, Skip, Repetition, Step

either

Lesson 27

① ② ③ ④ ⑤ ⑥

Lesson 29

1. Staff, 2. Treble clef, 3. Leger, 4. Quarter note,
5. Flat, 6. Whole rest, 7. 2, 8. Great, 9. Half,
10. Accidental, 11. Raises, 12. Quarter rest, 13 Bass,
14. Dotted half note, 15. Natural, 16. 7

ANSWER SHEET

Lesson 1 (More than one correct answer)

BED, CABBAGE, FED, BEAD

Lesson 5 — Ab, D, Bb, F, E, B

Lesson 6 — For answer, check against lessons 3 & 4

Lesson 7

Key of Bb   Key of F   Key of C   Key of B   Key of G

Lesson 9

1. 3, 2. 1½, 3.1, 4. 2, 5. 2, 6. ½, 7. 3, 8. 2

Lesson 10

1. d., 2. 4/4, 3. o·, 4. 2, 5. ♪, 6. 4

Lesson 11

Lesson 12 — 1. d., 2. d·, 3. 6/8, 4. 6/8, 5. 3/4, 3/2.
6. d, 7. C or 4/4, 8. 6/8, 9. d., 10. 6/8 11. 2, 4 or 8. 12. cut

Lesson 13 — 1. d⌣d = 3 beats 2. o⌣d· = 7 beats 3. d.⌣♪ = 2 beats 4. d⌣d = 2 beats

Lesson 14 — Tie slur
slur slur
tie tie

Lesson 15 — 1. d 2. d·. 3. 4/4. 4. end. 5. d
6. d gets one beat, 7. beats in a measure, 8. o

Lesson 16

A

B

Lesson 17

Lesson 18 — 4th, 2nd, 5th, 6th, 7th, 3rd
5th, 6th, 3rd, 4th, 4th, 7th

ANSWER SHEET

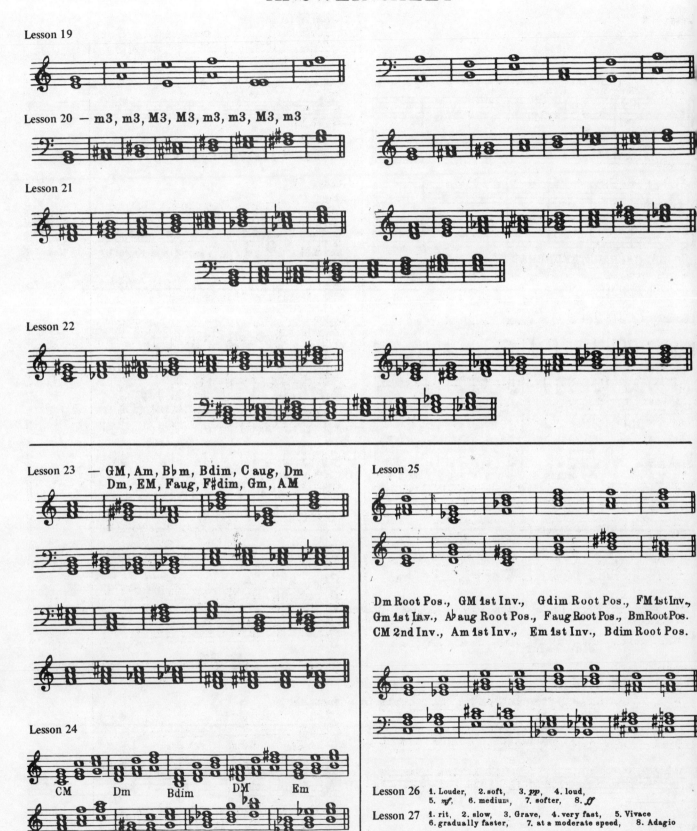

Lesson 19

Lesson 20 — m3, m3, M3, M3, m3, m3, M3, m3

Lesson 21

Lesson 22

Lesson 23 — GM, Am, B♭m, Bdim, Caug, Dm
Dm, EM, Faug, F#dim, Gm, AM

Lesson 24

CM   Dm   Bdim   DM   Em

FM   Caug   Gdim   E♭M

Lesson 25

Dm Root Pos., GM 1st Inv., Gdim Root Pos., FM 1st Inv.,
Gm 1st Inv., A♭ aug Root Pos., Faug Root Pos., Bm Root Pos.,
CM 2nd Inv., Am 1st Inv., Em 1st Inv., Bdim Root Pos.

Lesson 26 1. Louder, 2. soft, 3. *pp*, 4. loud,
5. *mf*, 6. medium, 7. softer, 8. *ff*

Lesson 27 1. rit, 2. slow, 3. Grave, 4. very fast, 5. Vivace
6. gradually faster, 7. at a moderate speed, 8. Adagio

Lesson 29 1. -d, 2. -o, 3. -g, 4. -j, 5. -l, 6. -i, 7. -c, 8. -a
9. -b, 10. -e, 11. -h, 12. -p, 13. -n, 14. -k, 15. -m, 16. -f

ANSWER SHEET

Lesson 1
A, B, D, E, B, E, A, F, C, B, E, D, C, F, C

Lesson 2
1. 2,   2. 1,   3. 1,   4. 1½,   5. 1,
6. 2,   7. 2,   8. 1,   9. 3,   10. 4

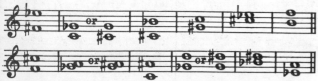

Lesson 3
1. 6/8,   2. 9/8,   3. 3/4,   4. 12/8   5. 3/8

Lesson 5

(rhythm notation)

Lesson 6

(music notation)

4th, Octave, Prime, 5th, 4th, 5th

Lesson 7

(music notation)

Maj., min., min., Perf., Maj., Perf., Maj., min.

Lesson 8

(music notation)

Lesson 9
1. Diminished, 2. minor, 3. Perfect, 4. dim 5th, 5. Maj 6th,
6. Aug 2nd, 7. min 3rd, 8. min 2nd, 9. Maj 3rd, 10. Perf 4th,

Lesson 10
Maj 3rd, min 7th, Aug 4th, Maj 6th, Perf 4th, min 2nd,
min 6th, dim 5th, Maj 2nd, Maj 7th, min 3rd, dim 7th

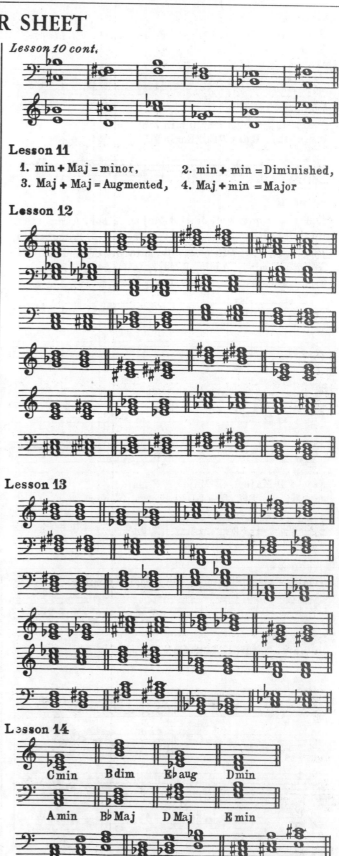

Lesson 10 cont.

(music notation)

Lesson 11
1. min + Maj = minor,   2. min + min = Diminished,
3. Maj + Maj = Augmented,   4. Maj + min = Major

Lesson 12

(music notation)

Lesson 13

(music notation)

Lesson 14

(music notation)
C min   B dim   Eb aug   D min
A min   Bb Maj   D Maj   E min

(music notation)

G min 1st Inv., D Maj 2nd Inv., B dim Root Pos., A Maj 2nd Inv.,
Eb Aug 1st Inv.,   Bb Maj 1st Inv.,   E min 2nd Inv.,
F Aug 2nd Inv.,   Bb min Root Pos.,   A dim Root Pos.

ANSWER SHEET

Lesson 15
G Maj 7th,   G (Dom) 7th,   F (Dom) 7th,   C Maj 7th,
E (Dom) 7th,   F Maj 7th

Lesson 16
A min 7th,   C# dim 7th,   G min 7th,
D min 7th,   B dim 7th,   E min 7th

Lesson 18
1. 3;   2. Root, 3rd, 5th;   3. Major, minor, Augmented,
Diminished;   4. min 3rd + Maj 3rd;   5. Raise the 5th;
6. Root Position;   7. Dominant 7th, minor 3rd+Maj3rd+min 3rd.
C# dim 7, E min 7, A min, D Maj 7, C Maj 1st Inv., B dim,
Bb Maj, F Maj 1st Inv., G min 7, C aug, G min 1st Inv., A (dom) 7.

Lesson 19

Key of D Major, E Major, F Major
A, Ab, B, Eb, D, F

Lesson 21
C# min, F min, F# min, B min, D min, C min

Lesson 22
Melodic, Natural, Melodic, Harmonic

Lesson 23

Lesson 24

Lesson 25

Lesson 26
A Major,   F# Harmonic Minor,
G Natural Minor,   F Melodic Minor

C Harmonic Minor,   A Melodic Minor,
D Major,   D Harmonic Minor

Lesson 27
1. Fine,   2. End,   3. ⊕,   4. Beginning

Lesson 28
1. B, 2. G, 3. E, 4. C, 5. H, 6. D, 7. F, 8. A

Lesson 29
1. X, 2. P, 3. F, 4. J, 5. O, 6. K, 7. N, 8. D, 9. S, 10. R,
11. G, 12. Q, 13. B, 14. A, 15. H, 16. T, 17. L, 18. C,
19. I, 20. Y, 21. Z, 22. U, 23. V, 24. W, 25. E, 26. M

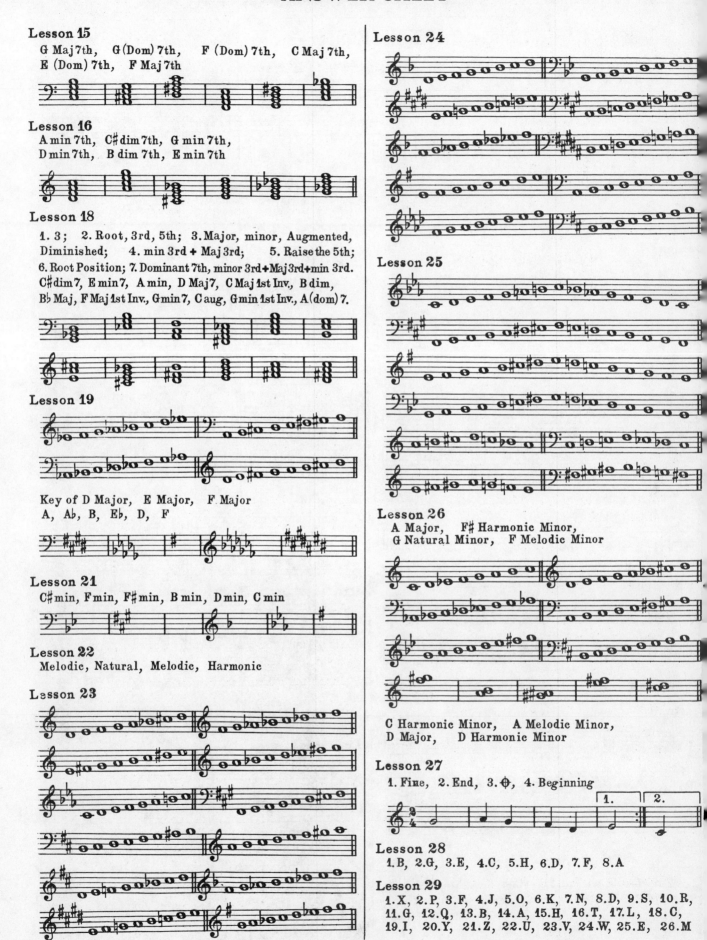